"FA NA BONA

JOBBA"

Do A Good Job

ANGELO LIGORI

FA NA BONA JOBBA: *Do A Good Job*

by Angelo Ligori

Copyright © Dec. 2025 by Angelo Ligori

ISBN:

978-1-998457-11-3 (Hardcover)

978-1-998457-09-0 (Paperback)

978-1-998457-08-3 (eBook)

978-1-998457-10-6 (Audio)

PUBLISHER

Prinoelio Press
London, Ontario
Canada
E-mail: prinoelio@yahoo.com

DEDICATION

To my beloved mother, Caterina, whose gentle wisdom and loving encouragement have guided me through every chapter of life. I cherish the memories of our long talks in the kitchen, your childhood stories that shaped my dreams, and the warmth of your embrace in times of need.

To my wonderful wife, Rosella, whose unwavering support and laughter have filled our home with joy. I am grateful for every adventure we've shared, from quiet evenings together to the challenges we've overcome side by side.

To my precious son, Daniel, whose bright spirit and curiosity have brought new light into our lives every single day. Your kindness inspires us to be better. Watching you grow has been our greatest blessing.

To my family relatives in Italy that have kept me grounded to mother earth in a way that brings me peace and happiness.

TABLE OF CONTENTS

PREFACE FROM CATERINA

Mom Caterina was born on March 5, 1933. She married her elementary school friend Giovanni in 1952 and brought her family to Canada in 1966. She is the sole person that I owe everything to. What follows are notes she wrote in her diary. They were written after she retired as a short order cook. She went to high school remedial English lessons in her sixties. The notes are not in perfect English and grammar to show her authenticity.

Mom's last entry is March 23, 2008. "Today is Easter Sunday. My children are with us. We all got together, and we were at the Ciociaro Club. John's parents, Andrew's parents, Rosella's mom, and a few friends are here. The food was very good. The company was even better. The day went by fast. Nobody had to cook for me. I really enjoyed that".

"Angelo is my first son. He was born on 1953 September 18, in the small town of Pofi, Italy. He was a boy everybody liked. He was raised at home with my father-in-law and mother-in-law. Everybody spoiled him in our house, and our house was full of people. I had three brothers-in-law. When Angelo was about six months old, my husband went into the army. He was in the army for 18 months. When my husband came home, my son didn't even want to see him. He liked his grandfather better. He followed his grandfather everywhere. His grandfather liked Angelo very much. Angelo was his first grandchild.

Angelo was never a baby. He always wanted to help. He started growing up on the farm with his grandfather. He was just three years old. Sometimes was a cold and rainy day, and I said, Angelo, you cannot go today. He started to cry. My son always had his own idea. Nobody can change his mind. When he started going to school in grade one, because those days didn't have daycare, kids started school at age six. Every morning, he got up on his own. I never have to tell him to get up in the morning. He always got ready for school on time. Angelo was a very responsible young boy. Right when he started the first grade, he became the teacher's pet. He loved his teacher, the first teacher. Her name was Giuseppina. He walked to school about himself because we lived very close. It was a farm school no car and no roads. I didn't have to worry about Angelo.

Angelo was very close with his uncle Luigi. He grew up together. Luigi was only 10 years older than Angelo. He was very good for him to play with when they picked him up from school. Angelo had a very good childhood. The grandparents spoiled him, especially his grandmother. He liked grandma more than Luigi.

The time went very fast. The school in the country only lasts three years, just up to grade five. Then Angelo started grade four in town. He still walked every morning with company, a few of the kids from the neighborhood. Even in the wintertime, he always walked and came home on time. He never did anything wrong to make me worry. He always was atop the class. All the teachers liked him because he never made trouble. I didn't know if he didn't come to Canada, where we would have been, we had no money to send him to high school. He was very smart, but in those days, just the rich kids were lucky enough to go to university.

Angelo took my heart away when he fell off his new bike and was in hospital for a long time. I thought he would not live after the first few days. I never forget that time. My husband lost his job to look after Angelo.

When he got better, we decided to send him to seminary to be a priest. Angelo was so sad there, and we missed him. He comes home at Christmas and does not go back.

When Angelo was 12 years old, we came to Canada. Angelo was a grade 8 student in Italy when we came to Canada. Because they didn't speak any English, they put him back in grade 5. We arrived in Leamington on May 8, 1966. The school was almost over just in a few weeks. Then summer is coming. Angelo took some classes in September.

He started to understand some things. He went from grade 5 to grade 7. He picked up English very fast, but for us, it was not fast enough because he never had someone to speak the language time by the time we started to receive mail. Every piece of paper coming, I expected Angelo to read for me because nobody else knew how to read. I had to write this book for him. If the phone rang, I didn't understand, so I called Angelo. He did everything for me. He was the man of the house because my husband was struggling with life in Canada. Angelo paid the phone bill. Angelo paid the gas bill. I remember a few times he came home from school; I always had something for him to read. Just went on in his room and closed the door. He put the pillow over his head and didn't say anything. Maybe he had a bad day in school. I never knew.

Angelo always was a very responsible teenager. He started work on the farm at a very young age and made his own money. He got older and had two jobs, one on the farm and the other one at the A&P, especially in the summertime. He was going to high school and going to university. He had enough money to pay for the first year and to give us some because we needed to pay for the house renovation.

Angelo didn't cost any money for us for years of university. He paid for everything. On his graduation day, my husband and I went to London to see him. He was very happy because he knew that he had done the things he wanted. He proved to my husband that he was in the right direction. My husband always said to him not to go to school and work at Heinz, but Angelo didn't listen to anybody. He had his mindset made up.

He graduated. Had a job in Sarnia, and I went to see him at the Refinery in Shell. He then met Rosella, and in 1980, on July 12th, they got married. They bought a little house in Sarnia. Rosella's parents were very good. They helped them out a lot. Sarnia's job only lasts for a couple of years. The company asked Angelo to move. He left Sarnia and then went to Edmonton. When they left, I felt I lost a piece of my heart. I cried and cried. I didn't want him to go away. Because I wanted them to be happy, I said yes. But my heart said no. I think now Angelo and Rosella had a lot of courage to move so far away. And they didn't know anybody. They stayed there for about 10 years, then came back to Ontario. In Edmonton, Rosella had her first surgery and had only Angelo, her better half. Angelo did everything on his own. He had nobody to talk to. My husband never said anything to them because he didn't know what to say.

I think he made a good decision to find a job in Cornwall and come back to Ontario. When he moved to Ontario, he had a job waiting for him. He stayed in Cornwall. Less than two years later, in 1990, they moved him again to Mississauga. I was happy because the first time I had the chance to go and see him. Only after a few months Daniel came into the family. He was adopted. We went to see him. I think Angelo wished that we had visited them more often because they had a new baby and the job that he had was very stressful. Because of the move, the job, and everything together, Angelo started to have a problem with his blood pressure and getting a little weight, so he started to run. Angelo and Rosella were very busy with the new baby. And far from home, there was nobody to help them.

A few years passed, and in four years, the company moved Angelo again. They are coming closer to home this time in Windsor, very close to home. I know it was a lot of work for them. I like it because we're seeing them more. Angelo had a much-stressed job. He traveled almost every week. He was going to the States first when he started because the company had a lot of work in Windsor. They were building a new plant. They made the Factoria a big one. And Angelo oversaw the project. This project only lasted a few years, and then the company started other projects in the States. This is when travel started. I don't even remember every week; he went to a different place, and Rosella was home with Daniel. She almost raised Daniel all by herself. But one day in 1996, she got sick. She was sick for a few months. She was in London Hospital for a long time and was just a few years old. Daniel was just a few years old. We always worry about Rosella, and she had a big operation. Angelo was under a lot of stress. Rosella's parents did a lot of work to bring her back home. Everybody helped Angelo.

I was always positive and believed that Rosella was going to get better, and she did. She came home from London. She had to stay at Windsor Hospital for another few weeks before she came home. Her parents helped a lot. Daniel was in the housework. Because Angelo had a job, they do. Angelo and Rosella went a lot together, through a lot together. But they were close to home. Rosella's mom was very strong. She went to stay with Rosella. She made sure that she ate well. She was coming out a few months ago and was able to stay home with Daniel. She sent them to school and cooked for them. In a few months, Rosella was doing everything, even driving a car. I believe it was a miracle for Rosella. Angelo and Rosella did everything on their own because we could help them.

When Angelo and Rosella moved from Mississauga very close to home, I was very happy because they were close to home, and it was very nice for them. Angelo traveled almost every week. I was worried about them always because he was there every week. Because now Daniel is a teenager better if Dad was home at night; that way, Rosella doesn't have to be home alone. He got a job in Chatham, so he drove every day, one hour each way. Angelo was happier than he's ever been. Last week, Angelo asked me if I minded going to the factory to see them. All day we had fun just seeing him. A lot of children were there for the open house.

Daniel this year is 17 years old. I hope that Daniel still will stay stronger and continue his schoolwork because he is a very smart young man. Next year, he wants to go to university. He needs another good mark to get to university. I hope that he can do well. Angelo has a lot to do as well because between the job and home and the family, there's lots of stress. He's a strong person around them, and I hope Angelo will make it through all this.

CHAPTER 1

Pofi Frosinone

Pofi sits on a volcanic hill that last erupted over 100,000 years ago.
It was founded by settlers from France in 416 AD.

The walls of what became a papal diocese are still there today. The town has remained at about 4000 people over the last 60 years as youngsters leave for cities or other countries. Our family was one of the thousands that left after the town was nearly demolished during World War 2.

The Ligori family in 1960 from left right has Grandfather and Grandmother Gaetano and Italia, Giovanni, and Caterina with Angelo and Anna. Uncle Antonio and Eleonora, with Cousin Franca are next. Uncle Domenico and Luigi are on the right. The four brothers had a feud with the Gori family below for their ent re life. We will call the Ligori's the Hatfield's. Mom Caterina was welcomed to the Ligori family because my grandfather liked her after I was born as his first Grandchild.

The Gori family above had a total of eight siblings, not all in this picture. We will call the Gori family the McCoy's. From left to right are Uncle Antonino, Grandfather Giuseppe, Uncle Domenico, Grandmother Candelora, Mom Caterina, Uncle Michele, and Uncle Antonio.

It was my uncle (Antonio) Tony who sponsored our family to Canada. I am told that my grandmother was the only one that liked my dad. To connect the dots, two families come together because grandmother Gori liked my dad and Grandfather Ligori liked my mom. Angelo was born from this relationship.

Uncle Tony married Zia Assunta and ended up in Canada by being sponsored by another Gori sister not in the picture. Pasqualina is the sister that got our clan to Canada. Of course, she came to Canada by another sponsorship done by the sister of her husband Giovanni Ciacelli. I will stop there because the chain just keeps going. That is how my hometown was nearly emptied out and Leamington ended up with many of us. My cousins from Rick, Elvis, Domenic and Carlo all went to the same high school and for year we were very close as most immigrants. Time and marriages blending into the Canadian way slowly moved us into our own lives yet we all still have that bond of roots from Pofi. Many have kept our roots as "Ciociari".

Now let's get back to April 1966 because events that make you are etched in the hard drive part of the brain and not ever erased. I was sitting crammed at the rear box of my uncle's "furgoncino." This cute little machine is a hybrid between a motorcycle and a car. It has 3 wheels and remains the preferred way to get around the twisted hilly roads. You drive it like a motorcycle, but the back side has a cube box for carrying cargo. Today, I was jammed in the cargo section. My uncle Dominic was the driver, and we were headed from Pofi to Napoli. Our family was going to Canada. In April 1966, I was 11 years old.

As I sat in between two luggage boxes, we slowly made our way down the bumpy laneway from the house where I was born. The bumps we not little ones, and the ride was a rocky one. The road was gouged out from the April rains. So, we were not moving at breakneck speeds. The slow ride allowed me to take in the full impact of my cousin Carlo waving goodbye to me from his patio. That image is forever imprinted in my mind. I really cannot pinpoint why the image comes back to me often in the later years, but it does.

Carlo continued waving at me at his young age of innocence. I waved back and him as tears ran down my eyes.

I was not sure why the tears were coming, but they were. Mom had told me that we were going to the big city of Napoli. I know that it was a big place because I had read about it in geography. That day, the curiosity of finding out about the big city was overwhelmed by tears. I was leaving my playmate cousin behind, and the big luggage told me that we were not coming back.

The tears were even more pronounced because the driver was Uncle Dominic. Now, I must tell you that he and I were not the best of friends. Our feud went back a long time. A long time when you are young is forever. He and I were at odds over a very precious belonging of mine. Yes, it is more precious than almost anything you can imagine. It is not money, and it is not replaceable. Yes, my uncle took away one of the most precious things you can imagine.

Italy is well known for its crazy shotgun owners. The Italians are known for shooting anything that moves. Any sized bird was fair game. Rabbits did not stand a chance even the tamed ones got it. In those days when food was not necessarily abundant, the need for hunting was there, but it did not justify my uncle's callous methods in my mind. Yes, my uncle shot my favorite dog Titto.

Titto and I were inseparable on the farm. We played for hours in the fields. He was my protector. I slept with him in the haystack. I rolled around in the hay filed with him. I took him everywhere. The best memories of him and I come from the times when I walked ahead of my mother to take her to the other side of the creek down the path to Grandma's house. Titto was the tracker and hunter of snakes. He could sniff them out in seconds. Then I went in with a stick. The snake would wrap itself around the stick. Sometimes, the stick was so heavy with the weight of the snake that I could barely hold it. That gave enough time for Titto to move in for the kill. We brought it out in the open, and Titto would bite it behind the head, and it was gone. Yes, Titto was my protector, and I was unafraid of anything in the woods. How could my own uncle kill my beloved Titto? On top of it all, he never told me about it. All I knew was that Titto disappeared one day. I cried forever. No one would tell me what happened. Finally, one day, Uncle Luigi spilled the beans and told me. Uncle Luigi remains my favorite to this day. Uncle Luigi is 10 years older than me. He used to practice cutting my hair while I held a bird he caught. He wanted to be a barber. We still laugh about those days. My hairstyle was very original and never evenly cut. It was the country version of the Beatle mania haircut.

So, with a man I did not like at the helm of a vehicle that was taking me to a strange city, there I was, crying my head off and waving at bye to Carlo. Uncle Domenico was the only relative that had any transportation bigger than a bicycle. We slowly made our way down the gouged out rough laneway of the farmhouse of my roots. The laneway ruts felt different than when I used to ride my bike down over them. Yep, that bike riding was also another memory of mine that flashed by. As we made our way past the haystack that brought back another ugly memory, I think I had every right to be in that teary state of mind.

We drove down the unpaved Via Forestella and went past the hose that had the only television in our neighborhood. Television was a luxury in the early 60s. We all went to Sebastina's house to watch soccer games and any special events. It's where I first fell in love with my favorite soccer team, Internazionale. That TV is where we all gathered to watch the JFK funeral. The room was packed with all ages and crying babies.

As I sat and thought about my experiences, these moments flashed into my brain. In the days of Innocence in Pofi, Italy, I had some fantastic memories of what you call young and reckless days. The daredevil time I recall going to the creek that flowed down by the hill of our farmhouse, and during the summer, whenever we had large rains, the creek filled up with swelling water. My buddy Luigi Scurpa was always with me. One of the things that we loved to do was to climb one poplar tree on one side of the creek. The tall, skinny trees could eventually weave back and forth. At one point of the swing, when we were right over the water, we would try and reach the tree on the other side. Every time we had that rain, we looked forward to doing the poplar tree jumps. One time, I did not hit the tree properly. I fell and dislocated my left elbow so that it went back past 180 degrees. Mom fainted when I showed her. The cast had many autographs of my school friends. I was the hit of the day, especially with the girls. Being 8 years old with a cast is so cool.

My best pose

One other adventure at the creek that was behind our Farmhouse was going to fish with our hands in pools of water that would be left over after the big storms each area that was a low spot would have a pool of water several feet deep. Our trick was to reach underneath and grab them with our hands. One time, I was grabbing for fish what I thought was a fish; however, it was an eel. Eels are one of the scariest things that you will ever touch, especially because they wiggle around and wrap around your hand and arm. That feeling is one that I will never forget.

Fishing experiences were also accompanied by one of the scariest experiences that I've ever had. On one of those expeditions looking for fish, I went in the water pool, and it was up to my waist. While I was looking for fish, I saw right at the corner of the bank that a water snake jumped in the water, and it was moving towards me. To this day, I have been so terrified of that sight. The head is up, and the rest of the body is waving around as an S shape with ripples of water following it. It was so scary. I got out of there so fast, and to this day, water snakes still scare me.

To help my fishing experiences, one of the things that we mastered was to have a bamboo stick and use one of Grandma's forks to put the fork at the end of the bamboo stick. With those sticks we were able to spear fish in the pools in the creek as well as frogs and any other animals that were in the water.

I also used that spear to have some fun with the sisters in our farmhouse. My sister Anna and Toni were upstairs; I was down below in a two-story farmhouse. The floor was old boards that had knot holes. Our fun was for me to be underneath, looking at my sisters on top. Toni was 2 years old and was particularly fond of bouncing around with her pudgy toes to make sure that we missed her toes. I was trying to stab through the planks and the knot holes so that I could hit her toes. Of course, it goes without saying that there was a little bit of blood, nothing major, however. Parents reading this, please be assured that we all survived. It's called the school of hard knocks. You will ask where were your parents? They were all in the fields harvesting crops and tending animals. The days of innocence with me and my sisters with my fishing spear with a fork remained vivid as we headed to Canada.

I love fire

As we drove down the lane past the family haystack, I must tell you about what it suggests. Yes, it was when I was young and impressionable. It happened one cold, windy day just before Christmas. What year I am not sure, but it was the year that "La Befana" did not bring me many presents.

It all started when Grandpa Ligori asked me to get him some matches for his cigarettes. Grandpa liked his "ALFA" cigarettes. He was just down the road at another farm, helping with the ritual killing of the family pig. Yes, grandpa was the town expert when it came to pig killing; back in those days was the ritual of a family. It fed everyone through the winter. Well, anyway, I got the matches from Grandma, and I was on my way down the laneway to bring them to grandpa. On the way, I got distracted by this nice pile of dry leaves that was gathered on one side of our laneway, where it met with the embankment of a slope that was maybe four feet high to the one side next to our haystack.

Those leaves were so dry and tempting. The matches were the long wooden ones that you could strike on a rock, and they lit with a big flame. I liked it when grandpa did it. I used to watch him all the time doing it. The match would burn for a bit after he lit his cigarette, and the coolest part was when he would bring it up close to burn the hairs in his nose. That was very impressive. I often thought about doing that, but I did not have any hairs in my nose. I wondered when I would get them. Maybe it was an older person thing.

For now, it was the leaves that I had in mind. I picked up a handful of them in my left hand. With my right hand, I struck the big match on a rock that was mostly embedded in our laneway. There are lots of them. The match lit up, and I brought the flame under the leaves I had in my left hand. They lit up like a flash. I did not have time to even look at them burn; I had to let go of the heat. As I let go of them, a few flew up in the air with a gust of wind that took them like flaming butterflies. Those leaves looked neat as they were lifted and continued to burn. They continued to travel over the side of the laneway embankment and into the side of the haystack.

Now, I must tell you that the straw stack was so dry that all the sides were pointy, like porcupine quills. The windy day made them sway back and forth. So, when the burning leaves hit the sides, there was a small pop that exploded into a fire ball immediately. Within seconds, there were several little circular fire balls at the side of the haystack. They mesmerized me as I looked at them. For a bit, I continued to look at them without realizing that as they got bigger, they were taking over the haystack. The circles grew bigger and joined together quickly. At one point, the side of the haystack was one big glowing amber ball. The hay was not really burning full out, but it was more glowing, and as the wind carried the tiny glowing ashes around, the glowing ball got bigger. Suddenly, it lit up into a giant fireball, and I realized that the haystack was engulfed in flames.

I panicked and started running into my favorite bush, where I used to play with Titto. As I ran into the bush, I crossed the path of several of our neighbors running to our farmhouse. I told them that someone had lit our haystack on fire. All the neighbors, along with the entire Ligori clan, tried to put out that fire but to no avail. When they found me, and I came back to look at it was a small pile of back charcoal. I recall the haystack being nearly 30 feet high. It was now a flat pile, maybe two feet of smoldering mess.

Yes, that year, "La Befana" did not bring much to yours truly. I got a red knitted sweater that mom had been knitting though the fall. She gave it to me because, you know, moms can't let their kids go without anything. From others, I did not get much. Grandpa Ligori was not a happy man that winter. We lost the entire straw he needed for the stable where he kept Stellina the Holstein cow that provided the farm with milk. Grandpa had to buy the straw that year.

Ouch that hurt

As the ride continued, we turned right, heading toward town. The road was wide enough to take 2 small FIATs but not much more. It was unpaved with the occasional gully and lots of rocks. So, as I bounced around in the back of the furgoncino, more memories were coming to mind. The memories came as I reflected on all the years of my young life. When you are 11, it may sound young to everybody, but to me, it was my whole lifetime.

As we made our way to a spot on the road about a mile away from my house, I knew exactly when we went over it. The boulder that I am talking about was big. At that spot, it stuck out of the ground by about an inch. It was flat and smooth from all the scrapings it received from other vehicles bottoming out on it. The reason why the vehicle bottomed out on it was because the rock itself was the peak of a good-sized crown on the road at that spot.

It was a sunny day, and on that day, I had the urge to take my nice new shiny bike for a ride. As I recall, I was not supposed to go out that far, as mom put it. I was still learning how to handle it. I was 9 years old. The air was warm on the June day, and as I went down the road and hit that steep bump, I lost control. The reason why I lost control I cannot remember because it happened so fast. I do remember hitting the brakes hard, and as I hit the top of the rock, I became airborne. I came down hard on my chin and my belly. I had no scrapes on my hands because I did not have time to even put them out in front of me as a natural reaction.

I lay there for a bit, and besides having lost my breath and bent the handlebar on the bike, I though all was fine. As I got up, I pulled out a small stone from the skin on my right side just over my hip. As I pulled it out, it started bleeding. As I noticed that blood, I also felt more of it coming down my chest. I felt around on my chin and got my hands all bloody. I put my index finger through my bottom lip, which was dangling to one side. I could feel my bottom row of teeth right through my bottom lip. The blood just kept coming, and my tee shirt was now soaked. There was not a soul on the road. I picked up my bike and started walking back to the house. It was the longest walk of my life. As I got to the house, my mom saw me, and she fainted.

The rest of the memories are vivid only in spots. They are vivid mostly because of the pain that comes with them. A man named Filippo, who had made money in America, had the only car in our neighborhood. He agreed to drive me, Mom, and Zio Luigi. We found out from the town doctor that he could do nothing. It was late afternoon by the time we reached the nearest hospital in Ceccano. At the hospital, I was taken to emergency, where they stitched up my bottom lip. It was raw. I saw and felt the whole thing with each poke of the needle and that raw pull of the thread through the skin of my bottom lip. The pain was masked by the other pain from my jaw that, by this time, was numbing. I spent the night in Ceccano in agony. The room was scorching hot. All I remember was the noise from the crowd watching the outdoor movies in the piazza next to the hospital.

Nothing could be done until I got to Rome at the Clinica Dontoiarica. After numerous X-rays that were all over the walls of my room, I went into surgery. I recall flashes of me with a full head cast that only showed part of my face. I drank from a straw for days. I got out in early August. I was kept in the hospital longer because everyone was afraid that I would fall again on my jaw. I cannot describe in words the pain and suffering that I put my mom and dad through. I was told much later that Dad lost his job while I was hospitalized. That experience formed my character and gave me the resistance to pain for the rest of my life. Physical pain, as well as mental toughness, was given to me at that time.

The Constitution

The Constitution was written on the side of the ocean liner that was docked at the port of Naples and being boarded by hundreds. The odd thing about the people that were boarding was that they were not all the same. There were beautifully dressed people with big white hats and nice-looking clothes. They spoke a weird language. Most were older and seemed much more occupied with themselves. They had lots of straw bags with them I did not see any kids with these people. They were all grown-ups talking in a strange language. Some smiled at me and talked in a nice, friendly tone. I had no idea what they were saying. "Sono Americani" said my mother as she held my hand in a tight way. Anna and Toni were on the other side of Mom, holding hands together. On the upper decks, more of those Americans were waiving at the crowd gathered at the pier. I am not sure why they were waiving. I am not sure why they were all happy and carrying on without a care in the world. I was making my way up the walkway on to this massive ship. I was curious about what was inside but crying as I walked. I did not understand why those people dressed in nice clothes were all happy and cheering. We left Naples that night, and as we headed out to sea, the lights of the city faded.

After a few days of stops in Genova, Cannes, Lisbon, and the Canary Islands I came to realize that we were on a cruise ship. Yes, the Constitution was a ship headed back to New York City full of American tourists with a bunch of Italian immigrants. The stops on the way were fun. We got off several times, and as kids would do, I had fun.

The fun came to a sudden end as we left the last stop and headed into the deep and rolling waves Atlantic. It did not take long, and the sea sickness took over. The food was already bad enough. The cafeteria made me feel a bit queasy even on the first day because the strange smells were not what I was used to. The food itself was all new. Even watermelon tasted different than what I had on the farm. For what seemed like an eternity, I was sick. That motion of slowly seeing the horizon rise and fall is etched in my brain. I ate nothing and spent almost the entire ocean crossing curled up in my cot. The Atlantic crossing on the Constitution was the trip to hell. To this day, the thought of a cruise ship makes me ill. One funny part of my ocean crossing was talking to the American crew members and not knowing any English. As kids would have it, I did learn some English. I learned to say "fuck" and "good morning". I often did not know which word to use first.

The sight of New York City skyline at night was fantastic not because of beauty and fame. I was getting off from this vomit hellhole. As we walked on the streets on the way to the train station, all I remember was looking up at the skyscrapers that went on forever. Even that experience was weird because I was still seasick, and the ground felt like it was moving. It's a strange feeling to be on land, looking up at tall things and feeling like you are going to fall.

The memories from the ocean crossing are food and language. When we got to Fort Erie to cross into Canada, we had to wait for a full day. We all went to a restaurant and there I got my first exposure to Canadian food. The smell was stomach tuning, especially after being seasick. The fries, hamburgers, and hotdogs were all new to me, and I could only pick at the fries. Mustard and ketchup were not ever in my diet, and it made me sick just to look at them. I could not eat until one day later when we got to Leamington at my Uncle Tony's house, where pasta was waiting for us. The train ride went on forever. It was in early May 1966, and to my disbelief, snowflakes were in the distance. Wait a minute! I was eating cherries 10 days ago in Pofi. Yes, the big, fat, juicy ones.

This picture was taken in June 1966 a few weeks after we arrived in Leamington. I am 11, Anna is 7, and Antonia is 3 years old. Mom and Dad are 33.

CHAPTER 2

Queen of Peace

It's May 1966, and time to head to school. Uncle Tony made all the connections and drove me to Queen of Peace School. I have a metal lunch box, a jacket with nice leather shoes, and a haircut. I was brought to Grade 5 and introduced to the class. I was terrified and sacred because I did not know how to ask to go to the washroom. The time in grade 5 was so memorable. I met Richard Gayer and Alan Tempich, who taught me my first English words. They both treated me as friends and ate lunch with me. Many did not and would always stay away, especially at lunch. My mortadella and fried pepper sandwiches scared everyone away. That summer, I spent every minute chasing friends and learning as much as I could. As time went on and I got my confidence I became a bit of a rebel. It was a time of missing my past and unhappiness. So, I rebelled.

I was lifted from a town that was 100% Italian Roman Catholic. The town of Pofi had four churches: San Pietro, San Rocco, Santa Maria Maggiore, and San Antonino. I was baptized at San Pietro parish and spent many days in that church smelling frankincense.

The sermons were long and in Latin. I still have "dominus vobisquom" etched in my brain. Leamington brought one discovery after another. The Anglican Church brought me my new friends. I learned that there are three school systems. The kids that came to school from the Mennonite community with blond hair and blue eyes were a novelty. The immigrants from Portugal, Germany, Greece and many others really opened my eyes. The first time I saw black families fishing the Leamington dock, I wanted to touch them so badly to see if they were real people. The Motown music, listening to Detroit Tiger baseball and following the Detroit Tigers was the beginning of my sports love. I had come from a one sport country where soccer was all I knew. The summer of 1966 was full of discoveries, and slowly, I forgot my town of Pofi. It was a time to fit in with no time to think about the past. In reflection those times made me resilient and expanded my curiosity immensely.

As it is with every one of us, we are programmed to see ourselves as perfect human beings. Some of us go out of our way to cross the line from decency to rebellion. That line crossing can happen from time to time to all of us, especially in our adolescent years. In June 1969, yours truly crossed that line. It was June, and we were getting ready to graduate from grade 8 and head to high school. I had great marks and was the captain of the volleyball and baseball teams, but I also had a chip on my shoulder and was bored. Remember that I was 2 years older than all the other kids. I was older and should have been more mature, but at 15, mature thinking did not yet exist.

Several events happened leading up to late June that would eventually get me expelled from school with 3 days left to go. In late May of that year, while playing our final softball game for the intra mural championship, there was a bit of a dispute between me and our gym teacher. I was playing 3rd base. A line drive hit was hit about one foot foul past the bag. I was right on the bag. The ball was called fair by the teacher who was at first base. There was no way that he could see it but that is the way that game was played. Mr. Miller was on first so that he could call those plays. By the time the ball was recovered by the left fielder, 3 runs came in, and the other team took a commanding lead. I lost it. I ran up to Mr. Miller and threw my glove down. I kicked dirt. I dropped several f bombs. Angelo was sent to see Mr. Brown. We lost the game!

A few weeks later, now that Mr. Miller and I were at odds, I ended up in the principal's office for throwing spit balls in his spelling class. I had a very nice story about that incident. I told Mr. Brown that I was bored. I was done with the spelling book since date April because we could work at our own pace. I was supposed to be helping other kids finish, but that got boring, too. Mr. Brown believed me and told me to behave.

The reprieve lasted a few more weeks. Mike and I sat across from each other at desks that were set up facing each other. Mike and I were best buddies, and we took our fun to class often. The difference between Mike and I was very evident. Mike was a quiet, shy person who would be any mom's ideal boy. That is why I liked him as my best friend. I think Mike must have liked my personality because we made a great pair. That day was typical. We were going on about something that I do not remember when I decided to take his pencil case and write in great big letters, "fuck off." Just at that moment, when I was passing it over to him, Mr. Miller happened to be looking over my shoulders and saw it. Hello, Mr. Brown. So here is the situation in his eyes. He has an incorrigible young man who has been in his office way too many times. It's a Catholic School. The solution is clear: send the kid home and be done with it. Otherwise, all the other kids are going to think that Angelo is getting away with it. So off I go home with this letter. I told mom the letter said I was so smart. I went to pick green beans at this farm where I was getting 25 cents a basket. The next day, I told mom that I was sent home because my marks were high, and I was done for the year. A few days later, this letter came in the mail.

June 25th, 1969.

Dear Mr. & Mrs. Ligore:

Due to the actions of your son Angelo over the last few days at school, we unfortunately find it necessary to suspend him for the balance of the school year.

On Tuesday, June 24th, he was involved in two incidents requiring disciplinary action. After the first, he was warned that suspension might be used and yet he misbehaved again.

I think it is about time Angelo's behavioural problems be examined carefully. He has a very poor attitude in school, he cannot accept the fact that he can be wrong or that he can lose and he becomes very depressed at times.

Unless he learns to live with himself, he will have problems throughout his life. I would suggest that you as a parent take a real interest in his problems and try to get some professional help.

Yours truly,

W.A. Brown,
Principal.

WAB/ss

My dear friend Mike Mastronardi is a civil engineer and partner in crime. We spent much time making gunpowder and launching rockets while his mom was at work. I am surprised that his basement made it through without any explosions. Many popular mechanics were studied in our formative years. One of the proud creations was our one tube radio that I listen to even today.

As I headed to high school, my mom was determined to become a lawyer. The job of moms is to set high standards for their kids. Of course, I had different ideas. To make sure that I was going to be a studious one, she followed up. The encyclopaedia Britannica salesman convinced her that we needed one for the children. I was the one who set it all up with a down payment and monthly payments made by money order. In 1969, we paid $359. I am sure that as you read this, you are thinking what did you both do? Yes, it seems insane, but also brilliant in retrospect. It motivated me in many ways. I and my sites used it so much in high school. The biggest motivator was keeping my promise to pay the monthly payments. Every month, I would go to the post office and send off the $25.99 money order. That discipline alone paid for the investment. At a higher level, I was learning to keep my promise that has defined integrity repeatedly.

High School:

I have told my suspension story to many. I link it to the fact that bored bright minds generality causes trouble if not harnessed to the fullest. I had a moment of connection telling this story to Mr. Brown. I wanted you to know about it, too. That letter was the catalyst for forcing me to rethink my future and refocus my attitude.

The letter I kept was the catalyst that motivated me in High School. I have read it over many times as a motivator and reminder of my battles with anxiety and mild depression. Truthfully, the discipline I got from Mr. Brown turned things around for me. In high school, I ended up valedictorian of my class because I put my underutilized brain to real work.

1974 was Leamington's centennial, and we all grew celebration beards. Mine made me look like a Cuban revolutionary. Smoking and being rebellious were the thing to do. The era of being cool by smoking lingered for decades. All of us smoked to be cool, and as time went on, we discovered that there is a price to be paid for all we do. I smoked off and on into my thirties when my first physical brought me to reality. Up to that point, I considered my body indestructible.

High school began to set me aside from the Italian kids in Leamington. The children of wealthy framers who came before me owned greenhouses and flaunted their wealthy and gold chains did not impress me. They drove up and down Erie Street with their Barracudas and Cobras whistling at girls. Instead, I was at Seacliff Beach getting drunk with Spike, Kirk, Doc, Dave, Herb, and Irv. It was all to fit in and have fun. This group became my safety net and defined me.

Mike Mastronardi was different as a friend. We related cerebrally. The others were my have fun friends. Mike's whole family was brainy. His two brothers, Louie and Jim, became my heroes of the time. Louie was an Electrical Engineer, and Jim was finishing up Chemical Engineering. My moment was the road trip to Queens University, where Jim was studying. The day I toured the Engineering Building; I fell in love with my profession. I never looked back and remember the lab rooms with glass, stainless and shiny everything.

After my Queens University visit, my focus on maths and sciences became an obsession. At those times, we were not required to take English. So, in grade 13, I took algebra, trigonometry, calculus, chemistry, physics, and biology. I aced them all, and off I went to UWO. In grade 13, I had a job at the A&P, working midnights and going to school during the day. I was in love with cars and bought a 1969 3 speed on the floor to be cool. I have regretted selling it forever, but I needed the money for university. I set my all-time land speed record on the Leamington town line with the needle pegged at 120 MPH. It was a rush!

1974 was also my first real job and a rude awaking to human behaviour. In grade 13, I was selected by Mr. Richardson to work at the Leamington Harness Raceway. I was asked because of my math skills. My job was ticket selling, and later, as I got better, I became a cashier. Horse racing tickets are simple looking but complex to cash. A day of racing has 10 races. Each race has 8 to 10 horses. A ticked has the date, the race number, the horse number, and the purchase price at $2, $5, or $10. Selling is easy because all you do is push a button. Cashing is more complex because a customer can have many combinations of tickets with race number, horse number and date. Customers are mostly gamblers and are always looking for a way to cheat. The customer area was well guarded by Security and Police. The one and only time I was taken was at the $10 cashier window. I cashed 6 tickets, and as I was recounting them and looking at all the symbols, I realized that one of the tickets had all the symbols ok except for the race number. I had been warned to look for anomalies. Normally people buy 1, 5 or 10 tickets. The bad ticket was over $50. I yelled at the police because I could see the customer, but to no avail. Lesson learned. As a student, I was given a warning and did not have to pay the out of balance amount. I later learned that at a larger raceway, cashiers had to make up any losses of the day!

The more responsible Angelo held a job at the Debergh onion farm. Here I'm sewing a 50-pound bag going to market on a nice summer afternoon.

Rene and Gisele Debergh guided me through the teen years. I looked to them as parents while my mom and dad struggled with finding their way to fit into the ways of Canada. I was faced with guiding our family at a time when I needed guidance myself. Gisele especially became my Canadian Mom and mentor. We developed a trust, so that I also became their babysitter. The children, Chris, Elizabeth, Lynn, and David, treat me like an older brother to this day.

The Tomato Capital Speech is the title of my valedictorian delivery in November 1974. Honored guests, teachers, fellow graduates, ladies, and gentlemen, it gives me pride and pleasure to stand here and represent the Year 5 graduating class of 73-74. On such a note, I will, as one representing the whole class, attempt to relate our thoughts into one message. We all must agree that Leamington District Secondary School has given us the most that we have in the form of education. Except for a few of us, we have all lived in Leamington for most of our lives. Every time we do some serious thinking about the past, our memory banks quickly flash upon those warm remembrances of the centennial town of Leamington. On a personal note, I would like to express a few ideas about our town and LDSS. It was here that my family roots were transplanted in the hope of finding bigger and better challenges. Here in the land of opportunity and equality, I have been able to partake in many activities that have been, to coin a phrase, super great. For every one of us, the step of leaving high school is a tremendously serious one. On entering the post-secondary institution of our choice, great amounts of mental pressure are placed upon us. In extreme cases, there are few who cannot bear the strains and tensions of complete freedom, resulting in a few failures in our scholastic achievements.

I feel that some breakdowns are bound to happen in the case of a poorly trained individual. Such an individual can be described as a type who has never been able to grasp the idea that conjugating French verbs and knowing that 1000 ml of water contains 55.5 moles of water is all part of our training, training our minds for the times of extreme tests. When one has mental discipline, he can more easily face the challenges of life, and only after recognition of a problem can it be tackled and conquered. Training of the mind through scholastic chores is, therefore, a tremendous stimulator that prepares us not only for the mental but also for the physical. Many teachers of LDSS across the province and country are performing excellent tasks in training the thinking processes of thousands of youngsters. It should be evidently clear that it matters little whether we remember for the rest of our lives that the square roots of a quadratic equation are always found by using a formula. It is that fact that our mind is trained to a further degree by the process of learning. Once we are out of the world of work or further education, it pays to have a trained mind, which we hope will never let us down. It does not matter how far away from Leamington we go. It's where we were trained for the big race of life.

All the people who contributed to building our minds here at LDSS are very capable individuals, including teachers and students. I just hope that my children will never come to a place like this. That's going to be the joke of the night, and I put it in here so that those who are almost falling asleep, it's for you guys to wake up. Presently, I would like to take a short time to recap in common the highlights that took place during the past five years for me. We've had a great many social activities with the entertainment, such famous stars as the Leamington Police Department, Dorian, New Potatoes, and the unforgettable Grease ball Boogie Band. Although I'm not very athletically inclined, it has been a pleasure enjoying the fine athletic teams that have represented LDSS. Sportsmanship, coupled with physical fitness, should always be regarded as a great contributor to strengthening the character.

So, keep up the good work, LDSS, and go, Lions! Academically speaking, our school was eliminated quickly when we participated in the TV show Reach for the Top, but the participants had a good time seeing themselves in the studio monitors for the first time. Rumor has it that this year, the school has won its first game. Leamington has given me much. It gave me my first scholastic achievement. It gave me my first pool game. It gave me my first cigarette. It gave me my first kiss. It has given me my friends and the chance to leave home for a while and come back. A little bit wiser and a little bit older. Yes, LDSS has given me the best five years of my life. And if this does not go through for all those other graduating students, well, they should have gone to Kingsville High. Seriously, though, before I sit down, I would like to leave all the graduates and graduates-to-be with a very appropriate closing statement.

The following poem is called If, written by Rudyard Kipling. I think it says a lot for all.

If you can keep your head when all about you Are losing theirs and blaming it on you, If you can trust yourself when all men doubt you, But make allowance for their doubting too; If you can wait and not be tired by waiting, Or being lied about, don't deal in lies, Or being hated, don't give way to hating, And yet don't look too good, nor talk too wise:

If you can dream—and not make dreams your master; If you can think—and not make thoughts your aim; If you can meet with Triumph and Disaster And treat those two impostors just the same; If you can bear to hear the truth you've spoken Twisted by knaves to make a trap for fools, Or watch the things you gave your life to, broken, And stoop and build 'em up with worn-out tools:

If you can make one heap of all your winnings, risk it on one turn of pitch-and-toss, lose, and start again at your beginnings And never breathe a word about your loss; If you can force your heart and nerve and sinew To serve your turn long after they are gone, And so hold on when there is nothing in you Except the Will which says to them: 'Hold on!'

If you can talk with crowds and keep your virtue, Or walk with Kings—nor lose the common touch If neither foes nor loving friends can hurt you If all men count with you, but none too much; If you can fill the unforgiving minute With sixty seconds' worth of distance run, Yours is the Earth and everything that's in it, And— which is more—you'll be a Man, my son!

Our First Date

It was also during April of 1976 that I went home for exam week and did my studying, and one of the studies was calculus. One Sunday, I went to church as I used to as much as I could back then to find peace of mind and soul. That day I saw the young girl that I admired for quite a few years in high school. Her name is Rosella. Sunday afternoon, I had enough courage to call her and ask her out. Mrs. Mattei answered the phone. I asked for Rosella, and in her usual Italian yell, she said, hey, "Roseh Telefon."

Rosella came to the phone, and we talked for quite a while; we talked mostly about school and what she was doing; by the way, at that time, she was in grade 13. I was in the middle of my cerebral times, and somehow, the conversation came up that she was having difficulty with determining how angles and geometry work. Well, I was right in the middle of math craziness because of all the studies that I was doing for engineering. For some reason, we got on the topic of angles. I believe the question was something like if Jack is on a hill looking down at Jill. They are 100 ft away; the hill where Jack is at is 200 ft high, and Jane is 50 ft lower. Can you calculate the angle that Jack is looking at where Jill is at? After a while, I did my geometry sketch back then, and we came up with an answer by Rosella writing out all those formulas on a piece of paper while we talked. I remember that conversation very well. Rosella still laughs about it; that was the beginning of our dating and, eventually, our life together. It started with the Jack and Jill story that we still laugh about.

A Solid B

Engineers and teachers are a natural fit, and so are engineers and nurses. And the way it worked for Rosella and me, a teacher, and what she was doing is a right-brain feelings person, and of course. I am the left-brain numbers person. After our first date phone call on geometry, we did end up getting married and had a wonderful time together through all the years. We always joked about the way she saw things and the way I saw things. She is the decorative one. She is the meal planner. She is the organizer. She is the one who always has everything neat and tidy. And I am more the geometrical get things done. So, you can see that through time, we have complements for each other. Later, as we got close, probably to our 40th anniversary, we had a discussion over rating me if I was a student. There was a lot of discussion over that, and it took quite a while. I got marks that were very good for outdoors and all the things that go into getting the house in. The property and the shrubs and the lawn and the garden and the mechanical things all score A+. However, in the household, cleaning, vacuuming, and all the things that generally require a little bit more patience and creativity, I didn't do so well. So, as it went, we went between an A and a B and an A and a B. It took a while. We finally settled on a solid B, as she says it. A solid B is a mark that a teacher gives to someone; if it gets to their brain that they're an A, they'll stop trying. And if it's a C, it's a little bit too harsh. So, after quite a lengthy discussion, I am now a solid B. And we've been together since. And as I discussed, we are now in the year 2024. So, I would say that a solid B over that period would be, I call it reasonable and respectable.

The Pink Panther

The Pink Panther dart was born out of another great adventure in 1976 on a cold February night. It was about 9:30 p.m. after a midterm exam at UWO. As I headed back to Adelaide apartments down Huron Street, I picked up a hitch hiker in the cold night. As I approached St. Peter's Seminary gate, a car pulled out of the gate, and I had no time to stop. I hit the passenger side straight on after a skid on the icy road.

I had hit two nuns coming from the Seminary. As we waited for the police to come, the hitchhiker stayed back to be my witness. I'm now thinking that it's my word against two nuns. It was my lucky night because Sister Mary told the cop that it was her fault because she could not see me coming over the high snowbank. That night was a gift from heaven! The insurance company offered $400 for the damage, and I took the money with gratitude. Keep in mind that I paid $100 to Mike Mastronardi's sister for the Dart. I considered this moment one of the biggest investments ever made. I went to a local junk yard and picked up a new radiator, bumper, hood, and fan for $100. A local garage put the car back together for $50, and I was off to the races. One summer job I had to do was to paint the yellow hood back to tan to match the rest of the body.

The paint job was done in July over a weekend at the Woodslee, Canada Agriculture Station after borrowing a spray gun and buying the paint at Canadian tire. As I started spraying the hood, it looked more like a pink skin color and not like the tan it was supposed to be. I carried on believing that after the paint dried in the sun, it would turn more into tan. The tan never came, and hence, the Pink Panther was born. By the way I started dating Rosella that April. I told her that I was driving a Dart, and she thought it was cool over the phone. When I showed up at her house with the yellow hood, she had a surprised look on her face but said nothing. Unfortunately, I parked on the nicely kept Mattei driveway and when I left a nice pool of oil on the driveway. I could see Mr. Mattei's face turn red as I backed out of the driveway. I parked on the street for the rest of the time I visited Rosella.

My experiences with older cars continued even after graduation. It was a beautiful June day when Anna graduated from the University of Windsor. I took the drive from Sarnia where Rosella was at work at Paisley photo studio. She had the new Grand Prix while I took the 1974 Valiant. The Valiant is an upgrade from the 1967 Dart. The Valiant was the cousin of the 1967 Dodge Dart, otherwise known as the Pink Panther. I picked up the Valiant from a retired couple for $400. It was an upgrade from the $100 Dart. I will tell you the full story of how the Dart became the pink panther. After graduation, I spent time with Mom, Dad, Anna, and John and headed back to on USA side on HI-94.

Just a few miles down the highway I heard a noise under the hood. It was the alternator that was seized. I opened the hood and noticed that the belt was hot but still turning. After a few more miles, I heard more squealing, and I stopped again. The heat from the seized alternator pulley was so hot that it burned through the main fan belt. It was a hot humid day in the 80's that day. I realized that without the fan belt turning the radiator fan; it would be tough to keep from overheating the radiator fluid. I was in the middle of HI 94 and decided to drive on. Sure enough, a few miles down the highway, the radiator boiled over and lost all the fluid. The engine temperature was pegged at maximum, and I had to stop.

In a moment of panic the creativity fluids started flowing. I found a beer bottle on the side of the road and filled the radiator up with ditch water. Off I go for another few miles until I boil over a second time. I let the car cool off and filled the radiator up again. I went another 3 miles. After doing some math on how far I had to go to Sarnia, I realized that at 3 liters per fill up, it would be almost 20 more times, and I would get home the next day.

More creative juices can to me. I found an old rope tied to the highway fence posts. I made and MacGyver belt that wrapped the fan pulley and main engine pulley. Thank God for no power brakes or power steering. Filled the radiator with water, and off I went. I got home in about 3 hours. With greasy hands and smelling like antifreeze, I was home. Now you all know why every time I see the picture I took of Anna graduating, I think of the Valiant trip.

Kirk:

Kirk James is by far my best friend and lifetime therapist, a partner in crime in so many ways. We met in high school. We drank Old Vienna beer at the Seacliff Hotel. We were work mates at the A&P putting totes in the back of cars. We played poker in smoke filled basements. We shared residence at the University of Western Ontario. The epic road trips to Buffalo to watch the Bills plays are lifetime experiences. All the things that we've done together, from me introducing him to his first wife, Cindy, and being asked to be the best man. He was my best man. I was the best man again with him and Caroline. To this day, Kirk is by far my most treasured best friend and will remain that way. We shared all the life precious moments. It was Kirk, knowing David Nash, who helped us with Daniel's adoption. We had many outings in Ilderton at his croquet tournaments. The mutual respect, as well as admiration has stayed with us a lifetime bond. There is no other person that has come close to my special friend Kirk.

We shared many, many classic moments. Kirk is the author of our Classic Creed. He was the mastermind behind getting our group together for many years, through the 80s and early 90s. He's now in Chicago with his family, doing very well. We've stayed in touch throughout. Even during my dark times of COVID, he was the one who called me and stayed up to recall all the moments that we went through together. He's helped me through. He's helped through visits, especially with all the times that we've had with Rosella's health at London Hospital. To this day, Kirk is the person that we have a great admiration for each other. I'm not sure what he sees in me to this day. However, Kirk, by far, is one of the people that changed my life right from the very first time we met.

Stories like this are the reason why Kirk James remains my inspiration forever.

The Philosophy of Pizza

Sometimes stories, and memories, link together in less than obvious ways. There can be multiple pathways to the same end, like a figure-eight *Fox and the Goose* trail in freshly fallen snow.

When the *Rumoli* game was over, I was introduced to a food that I grew to love – and still do to this day. Pizza! The Dutot (pron. Du-toe) family had just moved to Leamington where they discovered a restaurant – *Diana Sweets,* on Talbot Street. Diana's (as we called it) made excellent pizza pie that could be ordered by phone, then picked up and taken home. The Dutot clan enthusiastically urged us to try pizza as an evening-ending treat. Aunt Donna got on the phone and placed the order.

Dad and Uncle Ted drove into town to pick up the pizza. The extra-large round warm pizza, that they delivered back to the eagerly awaiting group, was delicious. From its thin baked crust, it oozed thick melted cheese and was piled high with cooked toppings – bacon, mushrooms, onions and green peppers. It was like nothing I had ever smelled or tasted before. Mom tried, but after that night she could never replicate the mouth-watering sensation of Diana Sweet's pizza in her own oven.

There is an interesting story that was running parallel to the *Rumoli* evening.

About that time, a lady had immigrated from Italy to Canada. Her name was Katrina Ligori. She and her husband, Giovanni, had moved with their four children to Leamington to build a better life for themselves. Giavonni found work at the H.J. Heinz plant in Leamington. Katrina took a job in the kitchen at Diana Sweets, working evenings from 4:00 pm to midnight. In her position there, Mrs. Ligori introduced some of the ingredients and steps that made Italian food so tasty back in her home country. In addition to the other traditional Canadian dishes she prepared for dine-in customers, Mrs. Ligori baked pizza for the take-out patrons. The delectable pizza we ate that evening was assembled, baked, sliced and boxed by Mrs. Ligori.

Now, the story jumps sideways into another lane but bear with me. The lines that might be dangling will reconnect, or at least cross.

When I was in Grade Six at Mt. Carmel, we had a teacher by the name of Stan Zadonek. Mr. Zadonek was of Polish heritage. He had thick furry forearms, like Popeye (one with a small tattoo), a rotund stomach and curly, slicked-back, black hair, shiny from an abundant daily application of Brylcreem hair cream (of the well-known TV jingle at the time, "a little dab will do ya"). His breath smelled of cigarette smoke and garlic. If he wasn't at school and was in the privacy of his own yard, he might roll up a pack of smokes under the sleeve of his short sleeve shirt, or have cigarette tucked behind his ear. On hot spring or fall days he always wore short sleeved dress shirts, but we had no air conditioning in the school, so he was still often damp with sweat. He looked like I imagined a Polish sausage might smell. Maybe even like sauerkraut, although I had no idea what that was and had only ever heard the word used when I was with Mom one time in the tiny deli corner of the butcher shop.

Mr. Zadonek delivered a no-nonsense, matter of fact, approach to discipline – anyone older was to be referred to "Sir", "Mister", "Madame" or "Miss", with the appropriate interjection of "pleases" and "thank yous". He would not have fared well in today's world of preferred gender pronouns. But he had a joyful approach to life and a great sense of humour. The kids liked and respected him. Mr. Zadonek wasn't married, but he struck me as the kind of man who deserved a nice wife. He was friendly, funny and engaging. He had a short stint at our school – I think he might have moved on to another township or county after a couple of years as his search for his soulmate continued.

In addition to the normal Grade Six curriculum, Mr. Zadonek was always trying to teach us life lessons. There were layers to his messaging, but you had to be listening. The majority of the guys in our class, eight in total – Tommy, Larry, Drew, Bob, Ken (*not* Ken Dick), Audi, Freddie (*not* Freddie Garant), Jimmy, and Andy (that's right – almost half of the boys in our class) – had failed a grade early on in school. They were a year older than the rest of us and were on the edge of their teen years, so some of them had some serious attitude going on. A couple should have been shaving – peach fuzz, mind you, but an unkempt facial look, nonetheless.

Mr. Zadonek took the older boys on as a project. He would often tell us real-life stories, imparting practical maxims while teaching a substantive subject, like arithmetic or science. For example, he might sternly appeal to us "Practice! Practice! Practice!", when orally testing our understanding of math equations. Or he might lecture someone who was drowsy with "Early to bed, early to rise!" His favorite exclamation was "Rubbish!", a word he delivered with relish to admonish us, sometimes several times in one day, usually when one of the older guys offered some lame excuse for not having their homework done or refusing to pay attention.

On a couple of occasions, Mr. Zadonek threw up his arms in frustration. Exasperated by our lack of interest or effort, he bemoaned the fact that because we were not motivated, we might never amount to anything. He spoke proudly about another kid he had taught at his last school, in town. The young man – his name was Angelo – had come from Italy and was put back two grades because he could not speak English. However, with hard work and discipline, in the span of two years Angelo had mastered all the subjects and risen to the top of his class. Mr. Zadonek emphasized that although Angelo faced language and economic barriers, he was always eager to learn and was respectful of those in authority.

Three years later, when I entered Grade Nine in high school, I met that kid who had immigrated from Italy with his family. Over the course of high school, Angelo and I became fast friends. Our bond grew stronger as roommates through university and, later, as best man in each other's wedding. Angelo is the son of Katrina Ligori, the lady who was the pizza maker at *Diana Sweets*, and the one student that Mr. Zadonek held up to us as an exemplary model of discipline and studious behavior!

As the years passed, I developed a deep appreciation for Mrs. Ligori – her work ethic, her industriousness, and her devotion to her family. I learned by watching her. Angelo's father, Giovanni, was a dedicated family man and hard-working too. Angelo fell not far from those trees.

Mrs. Ligori, and the delicious pizza she could make from scratch, personified a winning philosophy for life. The ingredients can be unpredictable, for sure. But challenges can be transformed into opportunities. Flour, grated cheese, mushrooms and pepperoni might look like a chaotic mess on a countertop. But you can make something delicious if you dedicate yourself and put it all together with an end vision in mind.

n '69 we loved our mothers
But searched for what we should learn to love.

She was petite,
but when her pride touched her son,
I felt taller too.

Her name was Caterina.
It made me think of a Russian ballerina
or an Austrian Princess,
but, in truth,
she was more graceful and regal even then –
in life.

Her smiling eyes were bright and told the truth,
but always listening.
You could see your soul in their mirror.

Her soprano voice was soft,
But measured and deliberate,
Their names her punctuation.
The cadence of a dove's cooo.

Her hands were strong, but gentle.
They kneaded chimella braids,
Folded line-dried air fresh T-shirts,
Peeled a half-dozen ripe tomatoes from the garden.

She sheltered her children.
She forged their steel.
She carried her faith and the old country with her, and in her.

I picture her shining – bashful giggling,
her affection for a young Giovanni.
Sixty-four years, one.

All of these things I saw or felt.

It was 1969.
We were young, and searching.

Her name was Caterina.
But I called her Mrs. Ligori.

This picture is a moment in time that was made to happen by my mom. She arranged a gathering in our backyard during one of our visits from Alberta. From left to right are Kirk James, Dave Tippett, Paul Taylor, Herb Kreling, Me, Jim Hillier, and Mike Mastronardi. We are friends forever.

The Creed

After graduating from high school, we formed a team that stayed together for a long time. We have stayed together and talked for many, many years and continue to do so. While we were growing up and having families, Dave, Rick, Kirk, Bob, Herb, Paul, and Jim continued to get together. For a while, we formed an annual event that had a creed that goes as follows. "I hereby acknowledge and affirm that money is the root of all evil, that age is a state of mind and that I cannot live with a woman, nor can I live without one. I recognize that there is a party animal wrapped in my body and that while I love my family, my work, and my country, I also love to go wild at least once a year. I acknowledge, invite, and accept my duty as a Christian. I am a Classic member for one weekend each year to recommit and return to a lifestyle that made me great. I promise to drink, gamble, swear, bullshit, carouse, and otherwise participate in any Classic activity, which is punishable by less than two years in jail. I pledge my allegiance to the Classic concepts that boys will be boys and boys will be boors, and that boys will chase broads, and that boys will drink; God bless the Queen, and God bless Canada. God bless Leamington. God bless Kate Smith. And God bless me."

The Leamington Classic group of friends are the backbone of a simple small-town life that got me through life and has kept me grounded. I have often been told that my approach to life, being grounded with common sense, is admirable. Once those values are embedded in your youth and observed by being around others, they eventually become part of your persona.

CHAPTER 3

The Hurried Decades

The Alberta experience was fantastic. Rosella finished her university with a Bachelor of Education, and she began teaching. I experienced colds, fires, and upsets, and I spent some time in beautiful western Canada and the Rockies and drove to Vancouver many, many times. And that experience, our favorite, was going to Hawaii on Ward Air First Class, which was quite an experience. We discovered West Edmonton Mall and the Edmonton Oilers because that's all you could do in the mid-'80s. We saw many Stanley Cups and Wayne Gretzky and that great team of the Oilers, and we went on a submarine ride at West Edmonton Mall. West Edmonton Mall at the time had a submarine fleet that was bigger than the Canadian submarine fleet.

In Alberta, everyone has a truck, camper, and snowmobile. Our camping trips with the Ruff family were so much fun. Every Victoria Day weekend, we headed out to Mirror Lake. Some years, the lake was still ice covered, and the mosquitoes ate us up. In Edmonton, we knew several types of mosquitoes, the small ones with a huge stinger. The big ones that looked like hose flies. The sun lovers came out in full sunlight. The ones that dive bombed you with jet propulsion all had reputations. Hot tub parties and ice fishing became our way of life. Welcome to Alberta.

Our time in Edmonton only comes into focus when I reflect on the historical significance of what we witnessed. The Oilers season tickets we had for several years gave us history in the making. At the time it was just fun and seemed that it would last forever. We witnessed the greatest team of the 1980s as if anything else needs to be said. The Oilers goal differential was +797, and they only played 800 games during the decade. They were the last great dynasty in the history of the NHL. We saw Wayne Gretzky earn 208 points, breaking the 200-point mark for the third time (of four) in his career; Gretzky remains the only NHL player in history to score 200+ points in a season. Winning five Stanley Cup championships in seven seasons was an incredible run, one that earned them acknowledgment by The Hockey News as the greatest NHL dynasty of all time.

Watching our Wayne Gretzky in 1984

The roster included five players who led the team in each of the five championships and later became Honoured Members of the Hockey Hall of Fame: Glenn Anderson, net minder Grant Fuhr, forward Jari Kurri, Kevin Lowe, and Mark Messier. Defenseman Paul Coffey starred from the blue line in the first three Stanley Cup wins, and Wayne Gretzky dominated in the first four of the five championships. We cannot forget Peter Pocklington, who sold Wayne to the Kings, as one of the saddest moments of our time in Edmonton. All the times we spent enjoying the Oilers dynasty seemed like another normal time of our lives. Upon reflection we were witnessing history in the making. History is only measured with time. No one knows when they are witnessing at the time. This picture below was published by the Edmonton Journal the next day. Its history now, but back then, it was just a moment when our friends called us to tell us that our picture was in the paper.

Alberta gave us a view of the west. Politically, it's conservative; at the time we lived there, the oil crisis was still dividing the country. Alberta had the oil, and Eastern Canada did not. We got to experience the famous Premier Peter Lougheed policy, "Let them freeze in the dark." The battle of provincial and federal royalties was being worked out, and Peter threatened to shut off oil flow to Ottawa! It was also the time when we bought our house at 16.5 % interest rates. We quickly fell in love with the conservatives when they gave us a $400 cheque mortgage subsidy. We loved Alberta right away! Our travels and experiences were at a perfect time of our lives. Leam and Elena had great parties. Rosella became close friends with Elena as a teacher for several years.

Leam and Elena made the best lamb with mint I have ever eaten! We are forever friends.

The Daniel Miracle:

In 1989, after waiting for years to go back to Ontario, we decided to move from Shell. I ended up getting a very nice job at BASF in Cornwall. Everything was going to be fine because I was going to be running a new plant, they were planning to build that makes phthalic anhydride. And no sooner did we move there that we found out that NAFTA took the tariffs away from the products made in Canada. BASF could make it in the US and bring it into Canada at no duty. We were so excited about moving that we had a new house built. We moved ourselves in the fall of 1989. We were all set up. For a while, we lived in a cottage, waiting for the house to be built. In early January, there was an announcement that the plant was going to close. I called Rosella and I met her at the cottage where she was freezing on a cold January day and told her that we would have to sell the house and move again. We were just waiting to move into the house, but the plant would eventually be closed. That was one of those moments where we both thought, what have we done? However, we didn't look back. The plant eventually ended up closing. I ended up being the person that closed because I was the last one hired. We moved into the house and rented from BASF. Shortly after seven or eight months or so, we sold it and moved to Toronto. During that period in 89-90, we also began a new chapter because during that period, we were able to adopt Daniel, and we had a new job, a new house, and a new place in Toronto, and that is a switch from Shell to a new job at BASF. Quite the experience all happened within 12 months. A new job, house, and baby put me in the stratosphere of stress level.

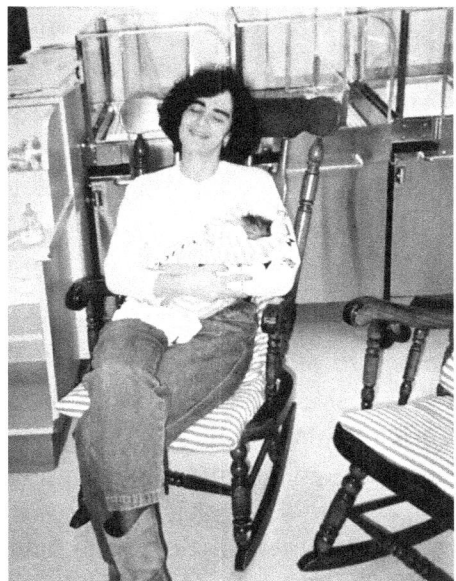

Rosella, holding Daniel for the first time, has a peaceful and happy moment that is irreplaceable as once in a lifetime.

One section of our life that changed us forever happened in December 1990, when Daniel joined our family. It started on the 19th of December when I got a message from Dr. Robbins while working at BASF. I said to myself, what does he want so close to Christmas? But I couldn't help calling him back. It had only been a couple of weeks since their last conversation, so I called right away.

The secretary said there had been new developments, and he would like to see us in London to discuss the developments as soon as possible. When I got off the phone, I knew that we were going to see Dr. Robbins on Friday, December 20th. I was quite sure about all the details, but I felt great regardless. The next day, we were on our way to London. We had talked by this time to our social worker who was working on our case. I got a phone call telling us that we were set up to visit Nash and Associates, who were making sure that the adoption would go through Dr. Robbins as quickly as possible.

Dr. Robbins called back and told us that, on December 17th, a boy weighing 7 pounds was born at Victoria Hospital. The birth mother has chosen us to be the couple that she wanted to give the child to. We quickly got some plans and decided to meet in Hamilton with our social worker to complete the adoption procedure. After we met, we asked our social worker if we could buy some baby clothes, and she said yes. We were on the road the Friday morning to see Dr. Robbins about 8:25 a.m. on December 21st. We got to his office, and Dr. Robbins, in very short words because he's a very busy person, told us the details. He said, "I have a baby." He's at Victoria Hospital. There's a social worker there waiting for you, so please go because your meeting is at 11.

We made our way through many floors and tunnels and the maze of elevators at the hospital.

We got to the west wing of the nursery section and looked in the baby room and all we could see was a whole bunch of bundles, some pink, some blue. It looked like it had been a busy place. For a moment, we felt like very proud parents. We were checked through by the nurses to make sure that we were the right people and went in to see our son for the first time. We were both there to hold the baby. We didn't know what to do. We studied his face. We started.

We stared and started to think about names because it felt odd holding a baby without a name that we wanted. We wanted to decide as soon as we could. But for now, regardless, it was a special time for us to be there sharing that moment. We went to the lawyer's office to file laws. However, we were told that it would take a while for Daniel to join us. And for the time being, he would be going to a foster home. It was the Christmas period, and things always take longer.

I went back to work. And while going to a meeting, so many things were running through my mind. I could recall this would be... What athletes call a "white moment". The white moment is when the fruits of all the hard work are paid off, and you feel that you've achieved and gotten all the things that you've always wanted. It's victory. You feel unbeatable. For a while, I felt like I was taken from Earth and gone to a place where I could never go back to. It's hard to be there forever. That is when something great has happened to you. I drove and cried with tears of joy, and I hadn't had tears for a long time.

On the 24th of December, we met with a social worker to finalize all the paperwork, and at that time, we got stories from the birth parents, a confirmation that Daniel was coming with us coming us from a very gifted couple, and we felt very special to have him at Christmas. Not all the documents were being finalized. We were quite sure that Daniel would be ours. We missed Daniel when we went back and held him for a long time at the hospital. We saw him just after he had had a bath, and he was still shivering, but we held him tight and warmed him up. We were excited because soon he would be coming home to us as a Christmas present.

On the 28th of December, we went to see Daniel with the hope that we would come home, and we could keep him forever. The lawyer joined us and told us that that was one of the fastest adoptions that ever went through. We signed six documents that would be needed to make Daniel officially ours. The name Daniel came this way. While we were doing all our travels at the Delta Meadow Vale, Rosella, after she came out of the shower, looked at me and said, we now have our name. It's going to be Daniel Brandon Ligori. That's the first time that we officialised it, and it was at a hotel. I know exactly where we both were. That's a special moment that stays with me for a long time.

After signing the papers with the lawyer, David Nash, we bundled him up in the car seat and drove through the subdivision on the way home to take him with us with tears of happiness. We knew that we were taking Daniel to meet the grandparents and the rest of the family and looking for so many great things to happen. On the way home, we were so nervous. He was in the back of the baby crib. And our first experience was I panicked. I had to stop at McDonald's along the 401, woke him up, take him in, and give him some formula, he was all sweaty because we had him bundled up with so many clothes just to make sure that everything would be okay.

A recap of 1990 was a very, very eventful year. In January, the plant where I was working was closed. In March, we moved to a new house in Ingleside. In April, we sold the house. In December, we got Daniel. On December 31st, we closed the deal on the new house in Mississauga. 1990 will be a memorable year for us for a long time.

Run Baby Run

After the life changing moment with Rosella and the Dr. Spiro experience, I went on to running with an OCD attitude that was probably dangerous. I had to make the change to make sure I would be able to look after Daniel and Rosella. I'm so glad that the endorphins changed me forever. We all reach a point in life where we must ask why we are here. What is my purpose? Why am I living they way I am? How did I get to be so overweight, and why have I abused my body? I reached that point in my early 40s with blood pressure ready to explode and 30 pounds overweight! How does that happen? It's by business travel, stress eating junk food, and an invincible mindset!

After nearly 10 years of a complete remake of mind and body, I qualified for the elusive Boston Marathon. On October 5, 2003, after 7 tries, I finally got my wish. I came in with a time of 3:34:28. I needed 3:35 to qualify for Boston. Right from the get-go, I knew I would make it. I did my first 3 miles at a 7:30 pace. I broke every rule about taking it easy. At ½, I was 5 minutes ahead of pace. At 21-mile mark, the 3:30 pace team passed me. At mile 24, I misjudged it, thinking it was 23. At the last mile, I knew I was going to make it. The last corner heading home into Ford Field was too good to be true. As I entered the stadium and saw 3:34 I had the most amazing feeling ever.

Here is my diary entry if you wish to read what goes on in the mind of an obsessed runner.

- Boston Marathon day of April 19, 2004, will be forever etched in my mind. The training, the pain, sweat, patience, and perseverance trough 8 marathons to qualify to get here have been beyond anything I have ever undertaken in my life.

- 4:45 a.m. – That's it! I am getting up!!! The day began with another tossing and turning sleepless night. Before Boston, I have run 8 marathons and before every race, when out of town, I have been up at 3:00 to 4:00 a.m. starting to put my bib number on. You would think that by this time, I would be over the nerves, but no. There is something about this race that gets my adrenalin going 2 days before the race. That night, it was Daniel with a stomach-ache as the reason for waking me up, but the result was the same. Another sleepless night. I said good-bye to Rosella, who looked up and said the usual what time is it? We confirmed again that if we did not see each other at the finish line, we would meet under the letter "L" at 5:00 p.m. She kissed me good luck, and off I went. I was out the door before 6:00 a.m. for a noon start time!!! It is going to be a long day!! I took a taxi down to Boston Common, where the school bus fleet was starting to build. During the taxi ride I heard on the radio that the temperature was a cool breezy 40 deg F off the ocean. I was freezing my ass off wearing a light windbreaker. The forecast was an unbelievable 85 deg F by mid afternoon. My thoughts were on the hope that the weatherman could not possibly be right. However, I knew that it had been over 80 in Windsor the day before, and the wave was moving east very fast. I arrived at the pickup area as the buses were just starting to roll in. I was supposed to be on the 7:30 a.m. wave, but I ended up on the 3rd bus and left at about 6:30 a.m.

- 7:00 a.m. – Hopkinton was just waking up when we got there. Roadblocks were on the side, ready to go up, and Volunteers with their red jackets were all over. State troopers were beginning to set up. The athlete's open area was frigid, and the grass was wet from dew. It was a cold 40 deg F as we staked out our area. It seemed impossible that the weatherman was still calling for over 80 deg F. Shivering, we sat on a plastic rain poncho that Caroline had stashed away. Thank God; otherwise, we would have been sitting on wet ground. There we were, ready for a 5 hour wait. The people kept coming in a steady stream and staking out their little spot. Some had inflatable mattresses and even little tents. It was like a minicamp out.

- 10:00 a.m. – the heat was coming on; we were at 67 deg F. The wind was picking up. We had a nice surprise by meeting up with 2 more Windsor area runners. Renee Scriver and Michelle Peuget-Peters just happened to be there. The sunscreen was going. The Gatorade drinking continued, and I had a nice snack with a bagel, cereal, banana, and coffee. There were people from all over the world with flags and logos. Australia, Korea, Japan, Germany, and many Canadians. The highlight was seeing 6 US Marines gearing up with their 35 lb. backpacks. They were fit as hell and going to run the race with back packs on this hot day. Unbelievable and humbling.

- 11:30 am – It was now show-time, and the heat had arrived at my disbelief. I finally wrote down on my left and right hand the split target times. It has been a tradition of mine for all other 8 Marathons. I saw no reason to break it at BOSTON, even though the heat was really confusing me. I waited this long because of the heat dilemma. The day before, I was thinking 3:40 finish; now I was mentally ready to take anything less than 4 hours but decided to go a bit on the aggressive side. The times were 5 mi = 43 min. 10 = 1:25, ½ = 1:47, 20 = 2:50, 25 = 3:35 finish = 3:47

- With a temperature close to 80 degrees F, we started to the athlete chutes. At this point, I had almost 2 gallons of Gatorade Aide and E load mix in me. It was mostly from the day before. I had Ironman cream all over my calves. One Advil and oozing Vaseline all over my body. I was wearing my favorite Canada flag singlet Saucony flats (on their last leg after running the last 3 marathons in them). These things, along with my adrenalin, were about to carry me to the finish of the most famous race ever for me.

- As we got closer to the start, the people were everywhere. They all looked fit and slim with that serious runner look. I felt like they were all ready to kick my ass. Caroline and I wished each other the best of luck, and I did not see her again. It was hard to get to my starting AREA 11 for my BIB number 11419. I got there at 11:55 am. In five minutes, so close to all the other runners, I already started to sweat. I thought about those cold days training along Riverside Drive in cold, snowy, windy, and just miserable conditions. One Sunday morning I recall the temperature was 8 deg F when I started one of my 20-mile runs. I thought about the 1000's of miles to get here, all the 20-mile long runs for the other marathons. I also thought about all the people who said they would be tracking me on the Internet. I did not want to let them down. Also, I thought about Mario Valeri, the one person who encouraged me to qualify after he was so helpful in getting me here. My last thought was I would likely not be here again. I must do my best, but I am not going to be a fool in this heat. I struggled with letting go of my "personal best" goal and continued telling myself to just have a good race. During the last few minutes before the gun went off, I covered more ground mentally than I would ever cover during the run. I was pumped!

- As the gun went off there was a loud cheer from the crowd. The Kenyans were off. I stood there in the heat with adrenalin flowing. It was showtime, but we had nowhere to run. It would be a while before the 11000 starters ahead of me would cross the start line.

- 12:10 p.m. - It took close to 10 minutes for me to reach the start line. We rounded the corner onto the main street as I crossed the start line and looked down the hill it was hard to contain myself from just turning it on at full throttle. The loud cheers from the crowd and the helicopters flying overhead made it feel like a dream. The first mile was under way.

• The hilly course gave me several views where the people ahead looked like a streaming and flowing mass of heads bobbing up and down due to the hilly terrain and occasional long stretched with slight curves. After the first few miles, I began to pace myself at about 8:30 with a constant reminder not to speed up. After 5 miles, I was at 43 minutes and right on target. This part of the race was so frustrating because so many people were passing me. I ran it all with 2 opposing forces. One was to speed up because everyone else was going fast. Two was to slow down because my better judgment told me to save fuel for the Newton Hills and the heat!!! What to do? I chose to keep the slow pace.

• 1:30 p.m. – At the 7-mile stretch, there was a long section past a bakery where we stopped, the day before during our drive. The crowds filled the street. Kids gave out ice, orange sections, icicles, jellybeans, and extra water; sprinklers kept spraying us. I got every one of the sprinklers. I took my E load every 3 miles. A second Advil at about mile 8. At this point, I felt good. I started getting confidence that today's heat was not going to break me.

• Nearing the ½ waypoint, we got a great boost from the Wellesley girls. Their roar could be heard ½ mile before we got there. They held signs saying, "KISS ME" and wore bikinis. At one flashing moment it crossed my mind that I should take one of them up on their offer for a kiss. Quickly, I realized that this would have been OK if I was 25, but at 50, I could be seen as just an old goat trying to get fresh. This logic told me that at the halfway point, I was still lucid. A good thing! All in all, the girls were a sight to remember and a boost that took me for a few more miles. At the ½ point, I was well on target at 1:53.

- Now that fun was about to start. I knew that just after the 15-mile mark came the first steep downhill. The day before, it looked scary just driving it. The hill did not feel as bad on running down it but the temptation to speed up was still there. I held up knowing that mile 16 had the first real big hill to test me. The famous Newton Hills were about to become a reality.

- 2:35 p.m. - The 16-mile hill was a bitch! But I made it all the way up. This was my first test at relatively big hills. By this time, I was down to a 9:30 pace but still running. I was just after mile 16 and one more Advil that I knew that I was not going to stop running today. I was going for it. I had this feeling one other time at Detroit when I qualified. Normally, at mile 16, one knows if a good finish time is in the cards or not.

- The next test was approaching mile 20/21 and the famous Heartbreak hill. I took it gradually with no pain. The day before driving it, it seemed so innocent. Today, it was quite different. I passed many runners cramping, stopping, and on their backs. One side of me felt sorry because I had been cramped up before, while the other side was more determined than ever that I was now headed home. Not stopping at Heartbreak hill was the biggest accomplishment of the race for me. This was especially sweet on this scorching 85 F Day when runners were falling by the wayside everywhere. Afterward, I confirmed that this was my slowest mile at 9:57. This section of the race will be a vivid memory for a long time. I am quite certain that at this point many people began walking for several miles.

- 3:15 p.m. – At about mile 21, just past Boston College, I had an 8:30 mile, passing people by the dozens. Here, I took my 4th Advil. Felt no pain but was determined to finish in style now that I could see the Hancock Tower and the famous CITGO sign in the distance. The finish line!! The pavement in some sections was freshly done, and I could smell the tar. My shoes felt like they were sticking to the pavement. I could not believe how hot it was. After mile 23, the water almost disappeared. I had to search for it in the hands of a few people in the crowd. The last portion of the run was dry as hell. My lips were parched.

• 4:00 p.m. – At mile 25, I crossed the famous ONE MILE TO GO written on the pavement. The crowds were screaming wildly and kept me going at a nice 9:15 pace. I was going home in tears. Unbelievable! I rounded the last corner and headed for the finish line on the famous Boylston Street. I could see the finish line logo, balloons, and a stream of runners ahead of me. It was at this point that Rosella and Daniel were watching me and yelling out my name. They say that I looked at them. I remember seeing or hearing nothing. At this point, I was in a trance. The sights and sounds I will remember forever, but there were no specifics. Just euphoria. Looking up at the cameras, I took my hat off and threw my hands up. Smiled and crossed the finish line.

• 4:15 p.m. at the Finish line - I broke down in tears. It was one of the white moments of my life. For a short period, there was a total feeling of complete perfection. The endorphins and Advil probably had a role to play.

• In a few minutes, reality set in. I looked down and saw a bloody right side of my running shoe. Blood but no pain. My feet were wet from about mile 8. I lost 2 nails due to the wet feet. No pain was because of the 4 Advil. My legs were now beginning to "set UP." I got my goodies and made my way through the crowds to the meeting area, where Rosella and Daniel joined me. It was a painful but great hour we spent there with all the other families enjoying the moment.

- 6:00 p.m. – I sat in the family section L for quite a while and enjoyed the moment. The crowds were hugging and congratulating all the participants. Looking at their medals holding each other. It was a real emotional time for a lot of families. I took my shoes off and let my bloody toes get some air. We slowly headed over to a Mexican restaurant where all the Marathon crowds were filling the place. I had a celebration been wearing my Medal!

- 8:00 p.m. – Back at the hotel, I took my ritual Epsom Salt bath and reflected on the day. I was so exhausted at this time that I just sat in the tub, replayed the day, and enjoyed it!!!

- With a finish time of 3:55:07, I was third in the Essex County group of 8 runners. To my amazement, I came in about 2 minutes behind the speedy Ed Oosterbaan, who mentioned in the Windsor Star he was shooting for 3:10. The heat really got him. I really had a nice day indeed!!!!

- Just past Boston College, I had an 8:30 mile passing people by the dozens. Here, I took my 4th Advil. I could now see the Prudential skyscraper at the finish. The pavement here was freshly done, and I could smell the tar. My shoes felt like they were sticking to the pavement. I could not believe how hot it was. After mile 23, the water almost disappeared. They last portion of the run was dry as hell. My lips were parched. The crowds were wild and kept me going at a nice 9:15 clip. I was going home in tears. Unbelievable! As I rounded the last corner and headed for the finish line, I could see the finish line logo, balloons, and a stream of runners ahead of me. A sight I will remember forever. Looking up at the cameras, I took my hat off and threw my hands up. Smiled and crossed the finish line.

- I broke down in tears. It was one of the white moments of my life. For a short period, there was a total feeling of complete perfection. The endorphins and Advil probably had a role to play.

- In a few minutes, reality set in. I looked down and saw a bloody right side of my running shoe. Blood but no pain. My feet were wet from about mile 8. I lost 2 nails due to the wet feet. No pain was because of the 4 Advil. My legs were now beginning to "set UP." I got my goodies and made my way through the crowds to the meeting area, where Rosella and Daniel joined me. It was a painful but great hour we spent there with all the other families enjoying the moment.

- NOTE: With a finish time of 3:55:07, I was third in the Essex County group of 8 runners. To my amazement, I came in about 2 minutes behind the speedy Ed Oosterbaan, who mentioned in the Windsor Start that he was shooting for 3:10. The heat really got him.

Boston Finish 2004

- OTHER BOSTON EXPERIENCES:

- Duck Tours, Tom Foolery, Sam Adams, Paul Revere, USS Constitution, Galleria Mall, Papa Razzi, Martin Myers, Suejeong, and Lily, who is 5 months old. Harvard, Boston Common, MIT, Big Dig, Exposition, Nice Jacket, Collector Finish MEDAL, expensive real estate, wild drivers, nice trail along Charles River,

- TRIVIA:

- Paul Revere did not say The British were coming. He said, "The regulars are coming. Back then, all were British. So, the difference was Regulars vs Revolutionary army.

- Sam Adams' beer label is Paul Revere. Sam Adams was too ugly.

- Bunker Hill is not where a battle was fought.

During my peak days of marathon running and triathlon days, I decided to bike to a 5 and 10k race that was held in Windsor. The bike distance from our house was about 20 K to get to the race. On the way, I was riding on Wyandotte Street in Windsor very early Sunday morning there was no one on the road. The lights are turned from red to green and back with no one on the road. I happened to be right beside a Ford F-150. We were beside each other for awhile because as the lights turned, the truck would go ahead, and then I would catch up. We did that for several lights until the F-150 decided to make a right-hand turn. At the very last minute, we were right beside each other. As the truck turned, I tried to miss him by breaking and turning. However, he hit me on the side, and I fell sideways. I was on my side looking at his front wheel that was inches away from my leg. I got up and scraped myself off. I could tell that the driver had alcohol on his breath; however, all I did was take his license plate number. I wrote it down, and I carried it on to my race. I ran the 5K and a 10K. By about 10:30 or so, my left rib cage was hurting so badly that I could barely breathe.

I mentioned that to one of the racing buddies that there was, and he suggested, "Angelo, you may want to go to emergency to get it checked out." I went to emergency, and it's now on a Sunday, very busy and emergency, and by noon, I am now supposed to be back home. I decide to call Rosella and tell her that everything is okay. I'm going to be a bit late; however, I'm at the hospital getting X-rays. At that point, I could tell that she was not receiving that news very well. I got my x-rays, and everything was fine except for a very small crack on one of my left ribs that basically must heal. They told me everything else is fine, you're in good health, go home. I did go to the police station, and I gave the license plate and all the information I had to draw out the accident scene, and that's all I did I'm hopeful that that person learned his lesson.

When I got home, it was now 4:00 in the afternoon. Rosella was so upset with me that I felt like a teenager. "What have you done? Are you OK?" There I am in my 50s, feeling terrible and not realizing that Rosella's eyes, I was way out of line! However, my mindset was," When I have to accomplish something, nothing stands in the way; no pain or person will stop me." It's very selfish and inconsiderate of those who love me. To this day, when I recall that accident, I was very lucky that that's all that happened. The truck wheel could have run over my ribcage!

I must include Mario in my story because of his support during the hours of running to get to Boston. These words are how I will always remember him. He is one of my lifetime friends who got my admiration. Our motto was "FA NA BONA JOBBA". Its Italese for "do a good job". It's become our bonding greeting that will stay with us forever.

October 2004 is the month of Mario Valeri. On his 3rd try, he qualified for Boston with a 3:11:10 at Detroit. I had the honor of running him in from Mile 20. The day was a great one for running. Low 50s, calm and dry. It started out with Rosella, Daniel, and me driving to Ford Field. After several detours because of all the barricades and construction for Super Bowl 2006, we made it to Ford Field around 8:45 am. Rosella and Daniel sat in quiet comfort, and I began my run backward on the course. I met people setting up the water stations at each mile. They were very friendly and cheered me on while telling me that I was going the wrong way. At mile 22, I had a beer at one of the cheering stations. The leaves were a great fall spectacle in Indian Village. As I rounded mile 21, I met up with the lead runner going in. It was about 9:45 a.m. He was a graceful strider from Kenya, of course. I continued to the entrance of Belle Isle Bridge, where I met Mario. He looked great and right on time at about 2:25. We passed the mile 20 crowds and continued down Jefferson and into Indian Village. Here, it was a nice run. Marion had a great pace and was behind me for some drafting. My encouragement was mostly about how near to Boston he was. We came out of Indian Village for the last stretch down Lafeyette. At Mile 24, Mario started smiling because he knew it was in the bag. We continued, and as we entered the last corner of Ford Field Mario was encouraging the crowd to cheer us on. He looked great. At the last minute, I exited for the stands, and he ran in with a great finish.

I caught Mario again after the finish and took this picture of him as proud as can be.

After the race, we stayed for a bit, then headed to Tim Horton's for a nice family lunch. The picture I took ended up being put in the Windsor Star by his wife, Diane, and Family.

CHAPTER 4

Health Surprises

The most significant event of my life started on a morning, having breakfast with Rosella before heading to work. She looked at me and said, "I see a strange image of you, kind of like another face, but it's foggy." She had trouble pouring coffee and walked very slowly, leaning on the kitchen counter. I called her later from work, and she said that her right leg was numb. I immediately took Rosella to a clinic. By the next day we had seen a specialist that suggested we go to London University Hospital. I have taken some sections of my diary that explain what happened next.

On March 6, 1996, I got up early and drove off to run a few errands at work. I left Rosella sleeping soundly. When I got to work, I spent about an hour explaining the situation to BASF workmates. Ron Barksdale quite understood the situation and said to take as long as needed. He personally had a very long experience with his wife Ronnie when his daughter Ashley was born. Ronnie was quite sick, and the delivery was a very difficult one. I signed over my authorities. Barb, our secretary, gave the name of Mt. St. Joseph's for a place to stay. I left the plant at about 10:00 a.m.

Rosella is the love of my life. I met her in high school. Afterward, we got married and had a wonderful life all the way to the time that she was 38. That was 1996. It began with a double vision and right-side slowness. Eventually, we had to have an attempted surgery that was not able to remove what's called a haemangioma. It's a benign tumor in the left thalamus. It's a very delicate area of the brain. After several attempts in 1996, it could not be removed, and the very high-end surgeons who did the work decided that it may be better just to leave her alone because surgery could do major damage. That carried on after she recovered all the way until 2011 when it acted up again. She had a third surgery to remove part of the haemangioma, but not all of it. The leftover was believed to be small enough that life could go on. So, we recovered and went back to our lives.

In 2013, it acted up again, and this time it started impacting very delicately parts of breathing and swallowing, which meant that the surgery had to be done because it was life threatening. The day I signed the consent to operate still brings awful thoughts to my mind. I was being asked to have surgery that may turn out positive or could make Rosella worse. Every time I recall this moment, I wish it would be different, but life does not work that way. The decision I made is the right one, and the rest is called life. Ultimately, I was deciding life for Rosella.

The final and fourth surgery was successful in removing the haemangioma. Dr. Gentili and Toronto Western Hospital, with his team, did an excellent miracle. However, it left Rosella slightly paralyzed on the right side and with a continued double vision. After all that, she is still with me. We are doing well. She is the hero of my life, for sure. I have learned so much as a care giver. My favorite friend is the laundry. It's always there for me. Even when we have a disagreement we must make up. Rosella and I joke about the laundry relationship all the time.

History was being made as I took the necessary steps to look after Rosella's life during her most difficult times. I am a believer that the actions we take give us results that must be faced head on.

My Heroes

The caregivers that have supported us over the years are so special. They are truly our heroes. Elise Dekker came into our lives at a time when both Rosella and her mom needed special care. Her friendly approach, lively conversations, and upbeat personality made our lives very special. Her support allowed us to get through some very difficult moments. Nicole has continued to be the companion and confidant for Rosella through many years. She has made our lives very rich in so many ways. She is a kind soul that has become our daughter in so many ways. Sabrina and Martis are the Personal Support Workers who help Rosella daily. Sabrina is always upbeat and brings conversations of what's going on in her life and it keeps Rosella engaged in daily life. Photos of the kids and stories about grandson Hudson liven up the mornings. Martis is the punctual and reliable PSW yet has such a sweet personality. On the medical side, Dr. Aggarwal has been Rosella's doctor for years. She's been a blessing because she's now not only a family doctor but a companion and someone that we can share some moments of life with. Dr. Liam is also a very special person who has helped Rosella tremendously in physiology as well as a companion. Overall, we've had so much support from Dr. Girvin and Dr. Hebb, neurosurgery, and staff at London Health Sciences. Dr. Gentili and his excellent neurosurgery staff at Toronto Western Hospital. Dr. Milan and his rehab staff at Bridge Point Health. Chatham Kent Health Alliance nurses and doctors have helped us tremendously. Our health professionals are true heroes, and without them, we would not be as well as we are. Now, it all makes sense why I have joined the Board of Directors and CKHA.

Mark Shuren

My famous bike accident that happened back in Italy has continued to give me surprises. Through all the dentists that I saw in Leamington, Sarnia, Sherwood Park, Cornwall, Mississauga, Windsor, and Chatham, I had quite an experience, and I baffled many dentists with all the dental work that I've had. Starting in high school, I continued to lose teeth because of the impact.

I joined Shell at Sarnia, and the first thing that any young engineer like me did I join the Industrial Soccer League. It was quite early in the season. I think I had just started my first or second game. I went up for a head ball, and next to me was big Larry Vadori. As I came down, he pushed me just a little bit, and I ended up hyper extending my knee as I hit a pothole in the field that was also being used for baseball. And baseball has those little potholes for the bases. That's where I landed. It snapped. It basically just gave me a noise that I had never heard before, and that was the beginning of my knee and all the things that I went through for years to come. It was 1978, and I was 24, thinking that it was going to be fine, but it wasn't. I went on crutches. I did some arthroscopic surgery, and one of my classmates from high school did the surgery; he said, Angelo, if you want to take it easy, you're not going to be going to the Olympics. Just take it easy. We took out a little bone chip. Then you'll be back in shape.

Then, as time went on, I moved to Scotford and Sherwood Park on the cold days. I played that period of squash, squash, squash, and squash. Jerry Ertel and I, my squash buddy, played for years, and I hyper extended my knee again. Because the squash and knees really don't agree, there's a lot of stops and go. So, I took it easy for a while.

My collection of implants and metal is a masterpiece of dentistry.

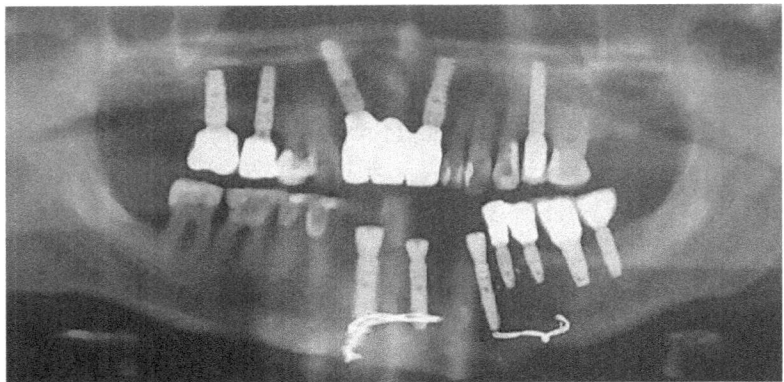

The wired jaw and 11 implants are one of a kind collected over 60 years.

The best experience is with my favorite dentist here in Windsor, Dr. Shuren, through the last 15 years. In the last 15 years of my life, I've had 10 implants of various sizes and shapes. The famous ones are the ones that were rejected because I have very little bone in my jaw, and I had to pull two of them out with pliers. Eventually, everything is back together, but every time I show up to a regular dentist, they look at my x-rays, the panoramic especially. Everyone looks at me again with a baffled look, wondering how in the world I could end up with so many different implants. It all goes back to that famous day in June back in Italy. Most recently, while repairing one of my few real teeth, the main nerve that senses tase was hit. Three year later my taste in almost completely gone. My appetite is minimal; food is now a mere necessity. It may explain why I can no longer put on weight. For anyone believing that weight loss is fun, my experience with losing taste is like the loss of a best friend. So, a message to all those who read this: if you have children and they have a bike, especially under 10, just be careful because this is the life that you're going to end up with if you smack your jaw.

I must explain that the dental surgeries and different feelings that I've experienced through painkillers and medications have made me wiser and allowed me to reflect on life. Let's go back to my experience with marijuana back in the 70's. It was a high school party that I tried along with everybody else that was at that party. The only thing that I remember is having a feeling of invincibility, and I walked into a sliding when it was closed. Fast forward to the age of marijuana legalization, and I was able to try gummies; all I remember from THC is having to look at life in slow motion and feeling invincibility. The medications that I took for dental implant pain, starting with Oxycontin, left me with a feeling of happiness. After taking three pills, it took me about 10 days to come off that feeling. It was awful. I had a crawling skin feeling when I was taking a shower. Each drop felt like a needle. That's all I remembered with oxy not a good experience to come off it. The next experience that I had was with all my dental surgeries. Tramadol left me a relaxed and numb that I could feel no pain and I could be in that mood forever; however, my ability to concentrate was not very good.

The morphine that I took for my knee surgery was also quite an experience because it made me feel hyper, unable to sleep, and unable to eat. Wired and hyper would best suit how morphine made me feel. For the cataract surgery, I took Lorazepam to control my anxiety. That feeling was one of happiness and inability to stop laughing to the point where my wife had to ask me several times to stop laughing. If I had one summary of all the medications for pain that I've taken, Lorazepam is the one that left me the happiest. CBD had no effect on sleep control. I thought you would enjoy hearing how I do with drugs.

Our Courageous Son

Sent: Thursday, March 10, 2011, 1:47 AM- Hey, Dad, so I'm afraid I haven't been completely honest about how things have been going these past few months... The truth is, yeah, there is a lot on my mind that's bugging me. I haven't been shaping up as much as I should... I still have that uncanny ability to convince myself not to do any work for days on end, and I hate it... I've been slacking off this semester, and I'm going to try and turn things around, but I fear it may be too late now... I think that regardless of what happens this year, whether I pass everything or not, it would be best if I took a year off... There's no point in me going back like this... I need to work on my discipline and keep focused on schoolwork. I wanted to tell you about these things in person, but the words keep getting stuck in my throat, so I decided to e-mail you. This way, I have time to collect my thoughts and express how I really feel. That night during reading week, I wanted to say everything: how I hate myself for not being able to focus on my work, how I can convince myself top just sit around and do nothing... I know you say I never will be, but sometimes I just feel like a disappointment... Like I've wasted your money on classes that I'm failing... I just don't know what to do, and I know that I've been distant lately, but I just find it hard to say what's on my mind... I think I really do just need some time to center myself and figure out what I need to do and where I want to go... I know I've said differently in the past that I've been in denial, but this is how I really feel. I just feel lost in life right now, and some time off would be great. I want to try and salvage this year but coming home after that would be best for me, I think. There are a lot of thoughts swimming through my head right now, and I don't know how to put them all down into words right now, but I'll e-mail you more as I figure things out. Love, Daniel

Daniel's birth mom selected us because when we sent our one-page description, one of the things that I had in there was that I'm an engineer. We found out by talking to our social worker later that the reason why she selected us was because she was in an engineering program when she got pregnant. From that point on, after the adoption and all the things that I, as a father, followed, someday I want Daniel to be an engineer just like Dad. However, what parents wish for their kids and what happens are two different things. As time went on, he did well. He has great math aptitude. He went to Western just like Dad. I introduced him to the Dean. I introduced him to the dean of engineering at the time, that had taught me. He was a young professor back when I was there. And I did everything I could to make sure that Daniel got through engineering. However, as you've read, one of the courses that makes or breaks engineers is calculus. And for some reason, Daniel could not get through calculus. In the second year, he had to drop out. And you can see by his letter that he was very disappointed. That was probably one of the most difficult letters that he's ever written. And I just wanted to share that part with you about what parents wish versus what happens. It doesn't always align. Now that I reflect on that, if you are reading this as a parent, please make sure that you have your children follow their dreams because their dreams and your dreams don't always line up.

Daniel dropped out of Engineering at UWO, and after a bit of time to think, we decided to seek some family counseling. We began to open about the future and look for ways to move on. Just as we were getting to understand the next steps for us as a family and figure out how to deal with Daniel's ADHD, Rosella required all my undivided attention for the next 5 years. To this day, I reflect at this time and believe that Daniel felt abandoned to look after himself. He worked at Future Shop and eventually decided to get his diploma at St. Clair College, all during the time I was looking after Rosella. He Graduated with nearly a 4.0 grade, and after teaching at the College for one term, he landed a job at Tec savvy in May of 2014.

January 4, 2013, we all signed this document as our Contract for Success

As a family, we agree to the following to successfully graduate Daniel with a Diploma from St. Clair College in Information Technology Networking. Here is what we agreed on to make sure that we kept our promise. Postscript: Daniel graduated from St. Clair College with 3-yearIT Systems Diploma.

Angelo and Rosella will:

1. Provide Daniel with $750/month.

2. Provide moral support at times when Daniel needs it.

3. Always focus on positive accomplishments.

4. Refrain from bringing up past things that did not work.

5. Always look to the positives that are in the future.

6. Wake up Daniel if he sleeps in.

7. Help with lunch if needed.

8. Remind Daniel of daily routines like laundry and looking after himself.

9. Have daily reviews of progress to look for ways to get better.

10. Remind Daniel of his medication needs.

Daniel will:

1. Attend all classes on time.

2. Do all homework between 7 and 10:00 pm.

3. Pass all courses with a 3 GPA or better.

4. Go to bed at 11:00 pm and limit gaming.

5. Set up a new and proper sleep and study area.

6. Provide Mom and Dad with daily updates with sufficient details.

7. Keep up the time and money spreadsheet.

8. Attend Personal coach sessions.

9. Maintain the car and drive safely.

10. Join a school committee.

COVID-19 Diary Entries - You Cannot Make This Shit Up

On January 21, 2020, Daniel called to tell me that he was sick with a terrible cough and nasty flu. He had come back from Ottawa after a week of work. It went through his whole apartment. Adrienne and Drake were also sick. Daniel came over for lunch the following week, still coughing.

On March 14, 2020, I went to the annual St. Patrick's Day 5km race in Wallaceburg. It was a cool, breezy day, and the whole race, I could not warm up. I warmed up in the reception hall with Irish stew, a beer, and about 150 people, all nice and close. Just over a 9 minute/mile pace is reasonable for this early in the season. The good old days when I was doing a 20-minute 5 km race are behind me. Oh yes, I was 38 back then!

On March 15, 2020, I visited my friend Enrico, who had his parents over from Italy. They traveled back to Bologna on March 16th as air travel to Italy shut down the next day. They had been here for the past week, having come from Italy. They were all fine and showed no symptoms. We did the usual Italian hugging to say goodbyes.

From March 17 to 20, 2020I planted 42 cedars along our property line. It took 3 days of digging holes in clay. It was cool and windy all 4 days. By the 4th day, I was exhausted. The dry cough started mid-week, and by Friday, I was coughing terribly and very weak. My legs were so weak that they wobbled.

On March 21, 2019, Rosella's PSW found me coughing again and finally convinced me to go to the COVID-19 clinic that had just opened. I went to the Chatham COVID-19 assessment center. I had a dry cough and aches. After 30 minutes of evaluations and basic cough tests, ears, eyes, throat, and medical history, I was not given a COVID-19 test. The doctor mentioned that I was in very good shape for my age! Got a puffer and was told to isolate for 14 days at home. The doctor said it's ok for me to be at home with Rosella and respect self-distance, like separate bathrooms and bedrooms. Lots of wiping down and hand washing. I was told to go back to the COVID clinic if my fever goes past 100 F. I was at 99 F when I went in. I was told that my lungs sound ok and I should be able to recover with puffer, fluids, and rest.

After the clinic, I went to Shoppers to get my puffer. The pharmacist told me to wear a mask immediately. They were painting lines on the floor and putting up social distancing signs. Below is a selfie at the clinic sign. Salbutamol puffer helped with breathing. The cough has slowed down but still feels congested. Temperature is at 98.6 F a bit of headache. Just feel like someone took a 2 by 4 and beat me. I went for a 30-minute brisk walk to get some fresh air. Its pajama day for Rosella, who is a bit tired but has no signs. We are wearing masks, gloves, and separate baths and beds. We are both emotionally drained. I have a feeling that it's only the beginning, but now more than ever, I will respect my 14 days of isolation as of yesterday. I'm looking forward to being able to go outside and thank God I have a big yard. By nighttime, I was exhausted. Rosella is fine.

During the next few days, I slept a lot with a fever of up to 99.5, a slight headache, itchy eyes, and a taste gone. If I talk, I start coughing, my lungs are heavy, I have back pain, I lost 6 pounds, I cannot keep water in, and very winded. Have a splitting headache.

On March 26, 2020, I went to the emergency at 2:00 am after my fever went to 102.5. I Got Fluticasone puffer and azithromycin for pneumonia. I was swabbed for COVID-19, and my chest x-ray showed pneumonia. The triage nurse, the cleaning lady, the doctors, and the nurses were all gowned up like a pandemic movie. It was very eerie. The long Q-tip up my nose was like someone was drilling into my brain.

On March 27, 2020, my fever spiked for a few hours back to 99. Other vitals are stable. Tired and short of breath. The doctors and nurses seemed to be confident that would be ok at home resting. I took 5 extra strength Tylenol for headaches over the day. Nurse Elise came to my rescue in the middle of the night to break my fever.

On March 28, 2020, the health unit called me to confirm that the test from an emergency was positive for COVID-19. Linda told me I was patient number 6. She also went on to say that my severe pneumonia could take up to one year to heal. At that time, I had no appreciation for what that would mean for me. **Postscript:** On December 28, 2020, I still have shortness of breath, my smell is flat, and I miss the fresh coffee aroma that I think will never come back. Aching legs are now part of me. That occasional dry cough acts up if I talk for a long time. Rosella hates it when I cough but likes it because it makes me stop talking.

While under medication and steroids in puffer, I wrote some bizarre texts to friends…. here is a classic for your enjoyment…. Mike: I tested positive on March 26. Still need at least one more week for a dry cough. In the last week, all the information about asymptomatic people has come out…. thanks to a fucking lot of health professionals. Today I took the Garbage out to the road….and that is all I could do before resting; I am so much winded. I can't taste food, so I can't put on weight. Hacking cough is insidious. Rosella is hanging in there. I will need at least another week, according to the health unit nurse.

Here are a second rant and rave to one of my sisters." The whole world has egg on their face. We as humans forgot that COVID-19 doesn't care about race, color, and religion. They knew in December that COVID-19 was asymptomatic and contagious as hell. No one listened because we were so busy. Sorry for the viewpoint, but that is how I feel right now. I just need to swear now; this is for your eyes only.

On April 3, 2020, I started a second azithromycin prescription. Out of breath, dry cough, no appetite. Want to sleep all day? Low grade fever persists. Health unit nurse estimates up to one month to get rid of pneumonia. Rosella has developed a cough. So how did I get the second prescription, you ask? After leaving 3 voicemails over 2 days with my family doctor to get azithromycin, I panicked and called Andrew, who is in my YMCA Spin Class. The person that knows everyone!!! I finally got the prescription from his dentist yesterday afternoon. Shoppers, a Drug Mart pharmacist, wanted to know from me that it was ok for a dentist to prescribe pneumonia medication. I said of course. Conclusion: My doctor is at the edge of irresponsible. I am going to drop him. Note: I did complaint about the CPSO. My complaint was taken, and about one month later, I received a letter from my doctor informing me that I was no longer his patient. Apparently, once the patient-doctor's trust is lost, it's normal to be dropped by a doctor. I was fired!

On April 9, 2020, the dental implant I had on March 11th continued to feel like a tooth ready to come out. After talking to the dentist, he believes the trauma made my body reject it. I pulled it with pliers on Thursday after the dentist said it would be ok if it got too painful. The dentist had a good laugh. It's already much better. That's $ 2000 but under warranty. Just must get drilled again.... this week was epic. As they say...you cannot make this shit up.

On April 13, 2020, I did a radio interview to share my experience with CFCO FM 92.9. As patient number 6 in CK, I was a novelty. By Cheryl Johnstone April 14, 2020 11:38 am

A well-known Chatham-Kent resident is sharing his story after diagnosed with COVID-19. Angelo Ligori is a senior advisor at Greenfield Global in Chatham and is known in the local running community for teaching spin classes at the YMCA. He started having symptoms on March 17 and went to the assessment center four days later, but he was sent home because he didn't have a high fever. Ligori went back on March 26 after his fever spiked. He was assessed and said the test was not pleasant.

"It's a long, long extended q-tip that goes down into, mine was in the left nostril, and they dip it down and it goes right into your throat," said Ligori. "It sits there for about a couple of seconds, and then they pull it out very slowly." Ligori found out that he was positive for COVID-19 two days later. "I thought, geez, I know I can just go through this. I have had other flu before, and you know I am in great shape. But this is a completely different animal. I tell you, the three days where I had a high fever, I thought, it is by far the worst experience I've ever had in my entire life." An x-ray also showed pneumonia, so Ligori also had two rounds of antibiotics.

"Some pneumonia cases have gone on for several months. I run out of breath going up and downstairs, so the thought it, COVID okay, say within the next few weeks, but for me to get my lungs back to do another, say, 10 km race, it will probably be Labour Day." Ligori's wife also tested positive for COVID-19 about 10 days ago. "She is reacted different; she's got a cough, and that's it. That is very typical of what everyone's heard; not everyone gets this the same way. I am a little bit older, maybe I'm a little bit more banged up, and it's taken me a little bit longer, but I'm back." Ligori said being in a decent shape helped him fight the virus.

On April 20, 2020, we received the best news ever. Rosella and I were both negative. I went to McDonalds and got a Strawberry milk shake, Big Mac, Large Fries, and Fish Filet. My appetite is starting to come back, but the taste is not yet there. Regardless, the meal was fantastic. I'm on my way back to gaining my 10 pounds. The health unit told me that it could be 6 to 12 months before my pneumonia symptoms would go away.

We celebrated by making a batch of Ciammelle, now that we have all kinds of time. They were delicious.

On May 5, 2020, after nearly two months, I was able to gout for a 5 km run, but my lungs were still not there. My resting heart rate is about 55 and not yet back to 51 back in February. My weight is 165 and slowly coming back to my original 170. Blood pressure is back down to 133/85 it peaked at 160/120 for several days in late March. My appetite is back, but foods still taste flat. I still cannot smell coffee. I decided to start eating as much as possible to get my weight back. A nice tub of Maple Walnut ice cream hit the spot.

My visit to the London Blood Donation Clinic in May was a very nice experience. It was for plasma donation for a trial to determine if antibodies that I have could be used to donate to hospitalized patients. Blackburn News did an interview with me. Nurse Marilee made a cute observation about my clear plasma. Apparently, the clearer it is, the better.

On June 4, 2020, Blackburn News was exceedingly kind to publish a story about my Plasma Donations. By Allanah Wills, June 4, 2020, 10:36am

A well-known face is giving back to others after recovering from COVID-19. Chatham resident Angelo Ligori was diagnosed with the virus towards the end of March. A senior advisor at Greenfield Global in Chatham and spin class teacher at the YMCA, Ligori was the sixth confirmed case in the municipality. Ligori previously referred to having COVID-19 as being the worst experience he has ever had in his life. However, now that he is doing well with his recovery process, he was inspired to help others who are dealing with what he went through.

Ligori recently donated plasma through Canadian Blood Services, something he was eligible to do a month after testing positive for the virus. "It's been quite a journey, and I decided to do something to help someone out," he said. Ligori had to go to London for the process, which he said took about 45 minutes to complete. Being a regular blood donor, he said donating plasma was a similar experience. "It is like donating blood; the only difference is there's a centrifuge machine beside you. It takes the plasma out and returns the red blood cell back into the same needle," he explained. "So, it's neat. First, you donate then feel this cool pressure stream coming back into your arm.

According to Ligori, the antibodies in the plasma will be used to help someone in the hospital who is currently battling the novel Coronavirus. "The idea is the antibody will help a person fight COVID-19," he explained. Ligori said he is well back to normal now and has gotten his weight back up to what it was pre-COVID-19 as well as got back his sense of smell and taste. Meanwhile, he hopes to donate plasma again soon. "I probably will go one more time," he said. "You can go to donate plasma every seven days. But it's up in London so it's a big affair for me. I'll do one more, depending on how things go." Ligori said the Chatham-Kent Public Health Unit closely checked and collaborated with him throughout his time with the virus. He added that it was his conversations with public health officials that inspired him to turn a negative situation into a positive one. "It's been a good journey and I'm trying to do something to turn it all into a positive because March and April was a pretty dark time for the whole family."

On October 3, 2020, I headed to London for donation number 4 and met up with nurse trainee Joel! This day was not going to end well when I saw Joel and senior nurse Michele scrambling around the chair where I was supposed to donate. Michele came over and asked me to sit and wait because they were trying to save the plasma from the donor next door. The unit had a power failure, and they had to spend nearly one hour saving the pouch manually. When they went to me, Michele began to explain the new COVID-19 plasma machine and how to poke my arm to draw the blood. She began feeling my right arm vein and explained in detail to Joel that he should aim the needle a certain way because of the angle of the vein. By this time, I could not look anymore because it made me nervous.

The two of them got distracted by the other unit one more time, and Michele had to explain my vein to Joel one more time. Now I was very nervous. In goes the needle and out came a shout from me that it really stung. After moving the needle around a bit, we got some flow enough to fill the 3 sample files. Then, alarms went off, and the flow stopped to the plasma unit. By this time, poor Joel was showing a sweat bead on his forehead. Nurse Marilee came to help. She was the one who told me I had nice plasma during my first donation in May. They tried to get the flow again but could not. I was told that they could not use my left arm for the program so out I went home without donating. The sample did show that my antibodies were still there, and I could go back again. I think I traumatized poor Joel after that experience.

I donated plasma 3 times since May; by October, I was informed today that I still have enough antibodies to continue in the program. I am the longest donator at the London office after 190 days. Nurse Mary and Michelle gave me the royal treatment.

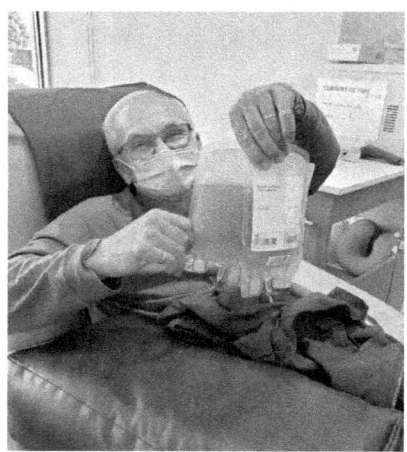

My nice plasma.

AFTER COVID: August 23, 2020

As I have done every Sunday for years, out I go for my long run. I turn right at Grande River and head towards town. I have a mile marker at every quarter mile so that I can judge where I am. I know almost every bump on the road. I always run against traffic because this road is narrow and has crazy drivers. Many will not veer away when they see me. Some that I know have not seen me will force me off the road into the bean fields. Rosella has hated my runs ever since we moved to Pain Court because of this road and not paths.

The first mile was painful. Legs do not want to loosen up and feel like logs. My pace is close to 13-minute miles. At mile one, I almost turned around. But no, runners don't quit. At mile 2, I began to loosen up a bit, and my heart rate leveled out at 137. At mile 2.5 came decision time. I used to go 6.5 or 7 miles in the old days, but my heart rate kept climbing, so I turned around and headed home. At mile 4, I began to feel a bit better, and my pace was now hitting 11-minute miles. Mile 5 got even better at 10-minute miles. I finished 6 miles, and it felt like a marathon today. I looked up my run from August 2019 and realized that I went further and almost one minute per mile faster. I now realize what the health unit nurse meant when she said that pneumonia can take up to one year to heal. I am still missing lung capacity. On the bright side, here I am, almost 67, and still out for my run. Hey dude, appreciate life a bit more!!!

Thank you for your help

September 20, 2020, was appreciation party time for all who helped us through our difficult times; it was time to celebrate. At 7:00 p.m., all our guests began to arrive, and by 7:30 on a beautiful fall night, we all enjoyed a bonfire at my favorite place by the river. Part of the celebration was the awards presentation to all neighbors and friends.

As usual, I had a few Angelo stories: Brian and Judee for receiving the Lasagna Award. They brought it over soon after I got my taste back, and it was delicious especially tasting the tangy tomato sauce. Susan received the Shepard's Pie award, which was accompanied by an excellent salad. Tom and Lorie's award went to the huge vat of chicken soup that was excellent especially during that period when I could hardly eat anything. The salty liquids helped very much. Enrico and Pat religiously brought us groceries for almost two months, and they received the courier awards. The world's best nurse award went to Elise for her medical advice to help me break my fever.

The absentia awards went to Andrew, the drug dealer, Carrie for best white pasta, and Kaitlin for best strawberry milkshake.

CHAPTER 5

Days of Peace and Bliss

These words are from my diary.

- Saturday, December 18, 2004 – FLY Day

I went for my usual 6 mile run down Riverside on a relatively nice day with temp of 40 deg F. We were off from the house at about 8:15 a.m. The ride to Detroit airport was smooth. We were at the terminal in good time. Our flight was full of families heading to the same warm place. Saw lots of kids and parents. Its totally different than business travel. We landed in Nassau on time at 1:30 pm. After customs clearance, we were outside on the muggy tropical day. As we approached the Hilton we could see cruise ships in the Harbor. The Harbor in Nassau is almost always full of cruise ships making their daily stops with loads of tourists from all over the world. It is quite a sight. Carnival, Disney cruise ships, etc., are all there. The Bahamas dollar is conveniently set the same as the US dollar; all money is totally interchangeable, and they speak good Queens English. They are the politest people I have ever met. All cars stop in their track when a pedestrian looks to cross any street. The downtown area has liquor, jewelry, Cuban cigar stores and street vendors all over. Every man drives a taxi of some form. The taxis come in all models. If you are not happy with a taxi, try a small bus. The driving is on the left-hand side on very narrow, crowded streets. Welcome to Nassau. My first night started with a nightly swim even though no one was outside on a rather cool 65 deg F night.

- Monday, December 20, 2004 – Atlantis Day

The morning run was indoors with a run, cross trainer, and bike. After a nice Big Breakfast at McDonalds just across the street from the Hilton, we headed for a nice long walk to Paradise Island and Atlantis. We walked through the gardens and to the beach. I walked all the way out to the reef and took some nice photos of the resort looking east from the reef with the beach in front. We walked around the grounds. Saw a shark pond, water slide, and casino and stopped for an afternoon cappuccino. Murrays Restaurant served us the rip off our vacation. For $25 US, we got powdered cappuccino and powdered hot chocolate. Daniel had to make it by pouring his own hot water into a cup. A truly low blow to the tourists…but they had us a captive audience. On the way back to the hotel, we stopped at the outdoor market at picked up his & hers fake Rolex watches for $175 US. We walked back over the bridge and go a great view of Harbour. Supper at Hard Rock Café was great as oldies from David Bowie, Talking Heads etc played on.

- Tuesday, December 21, 2004 – SNORKLE day

The morning run (8 miles) was to Cable beach resort hotels. The path is very nice, with more beaches to my side for almost the entire run. We spent a bit of time downtown before being picked up by bus to Flying Cloud Catamaran dock. The crew of 4 was very friendly.

They day was a bit choppy but sunny. We made our way east out of the harbor past the fishing and cargo ships. On the one side, we could see all the large homes on Paradise Island's shoreline near the golf course. One of the people on board mentioned that Barry Bonds had a home there. The homes are spectacular palatial estates. We got out about 10 miles, and the captain let up the sails. We wee really moving on sail power. The snorkeling was quite an experience. My breathing was OK after a couple of minutes. The view below was aquarium like. There were schools of fish moving about in all directions. The reef was a colorful green, blue, and brown. The bright reds did not show well. I went out for what seemed forever but only 15 minutes. The water chop kept getting small amounts of salt water into my mouth. After a bit, it became irritating, so I headed in. The other problem was the current, and the last one was trying to swim with a camera in one palm. As I reached the lifeline, I began pulling myself in and looking down a bit more. With the lifeline, it was a bit more comforting. As I boarded the boat, I realized that my wedding band had bleed donated to the reef below. It was probably tugging at the lifeline that pulled it off. I was pissed, to say the least; as I showed Rosella, she shed a tear. The bright side is that we would get a new one in Nassau as a memory. On our way back, the crew put on music, danced, and had a blast. It was a great outing. We picked up Daniel's Rolex at an outdoor market for a family set. Supper at SENOR FROGS was an experience. The food was so, so, but the place was a big party with an announcer who had people on stage for drinking races and no stop music. It is the happiest place for the Cruise ship rich kids.

- Thursday December 23, 2004 - SCUBA

The morning run (8 miles) was to Atlantis Beach, where I took my shoes off and went all round the small bay. It was a calm, sunny morning. The sand and water felt so soothing to my feet. The run over was about 4 miles to get there. I met up with a couple of runners along the way. Most people were still asleep at 6:30 a.m. I did the east leg to the golf course and headed back over the bridge down Bay Street through downtown and to the Hilton.

After picking up my new wedding band at one of the many tourist jewelleries we headed for Stuarts Cove for our Scuba Experience. On the way we took a small bus that was packed. We were the only first timers on the bus; all others were busy talking about their past dives. It was a bit intimidating, but Daniel and I were up for the occasion. After completing a ton of waiver forms and health questionnaires, we were finally on board the White Bunge. A young Calgarian was the instructor and hit of the day. Our first dive was instructional on the basics of getting water out of the mask, removing the mouthpiece, and recovering the mouthpiece. We got bravery comments for being the only ones without wet suits. We told all that we were tough Canadians. Wet suits are for sissies. The second dive took us down about 25 feet. It took me some getting used to the slow descent. I felt popping my ears several times on the way down. Once down there, it was a true experience. The numerous fish were all around our heads. It felt like you could touch them all, and yet they would move away just at the last minute. Daniel was almost always beside me. It was great to see him handle the water so well. He really enjoyed himself. At supper, we had a great night at the Hilton with pasta, wine, dessert, and a great talk about how great the day was. Closed off the evening watching Ferris Buller's Day Off and my evening swim. Temp at 9:30 pm was mid 70's

- Friday, December 24, 2004 – Heading Home

Up at 5:30 am and off to my morning run. This morning, I decided to first use the exercise room on a cross trainer and stationary bike. We watched the BBC with several Brits also on vacation. It looks like the Hilton is a favourite spot for them. I went out for a short run toward Cable Island. I ran back and forth on a nearby beach for about 20 min. The sun was coming up from the east, and it felt warm in my face. The water was calm and crystal clear. As I ran along the beach, I thought of the weather report from CNN last night. Detroit was under a blanket of snow with wind chills to Zero deg F. It was already 75 deg F this morning. On my way back to the room, I decided to go for one last swim in the Atlantic. It was very refreshing at 8:00 a.m. We all went down to Portofino for one last big buffet breakfast. The 3 of us enjoyed the moment and reminisced about yesterday's Scuba experience. We went for one last check out of the open market. We boarded the bus to the airport at about noon and said goodbye to the Hilton and to all the door men wanting us to come back to Junkanoo. Junkanoo is their big traditional costume and dance feast heal on 2 days. Boxing Day and January 1st. It is a celebration dating back to the slave days. On this day, all the slaves were allowed to celebrate and get together. Got home to over one foot of snow and barely made it up the driveway. Welcome back!

The time we spend with our children is always precious and stays with us longer. On our vacation in Cancun, we had a special time.

Daniel was old enough to hang out and not too old to say, "I have my friends now." It's a picture of contentment and relaxation that is hard to bottle up.

Our family travels continued to place that, at the time, were the thing to do. New York City was our destination several times. One of the trips had the harbour cruise that everyone must take. As we admired the breathtaking skyline, I took many pictures. The one you see is hanging on our wall as a piece of history. We never know when we are witnessing history until time passes and puts it in perspective. Every time I look at this picture, I think of the days I jogged through the Twin Towers walkways from our hotel on a quiet morning before the crowds. I can picture every shiny handrail and polished floor.

I am sure that every one of us remembers exactly where we were on September 11, 2001, at around 9 a.m.

CHAPTER 6

Fired

Mexico, here we come:

My BASF work assignment in Mexico City assignment gave me the opportunity to spend six months in 2004 in one of the wildest and busiest cities in the world. In Mexico City people live and party with passion. Work in Mexico City is a hardship beyond our comprehension. Most people have 12–14-hour workdays 6 days per week, making less than $10,000 per year. On Sundays or evenings, many people have a second job selling tacos on the side of the street. I met many people who left their houses at 6:00 a.m. to drive for up to 2 hours in the busiest city in the world. The traffic is not like ours. It is a mix of wild drivers, Micro buses pulling in and out, horns blaring, and trucks hauling loads so heavy that a gradual slope slows them down to 10 mph. Construction trucks going down main highways with workers standing in the rear box. This is what a worker must fight though to get to work. The return trip is similar starting sometime around 8:00 pm when traffic lightens up a bit. It is for this reason that a Canadian viewpoint that I bring quickly clashes with their everyday life.

As part of life as a business expatriate, I was assigned a personal driver. Miguel was responsible for picking me up at the airport and returning me there. He was familiar with the crazy traffic and made sure I was kept safe. Daily trips to and from the hotel were all with one of the BASF managers, who took turns. The drives were all an experience for me sitting in the passenger seat. One experience was following a stake truck with several young men hanging on to ropes that made a ring around the flatbed. It looked very scary and unsafe. Roberto Correa just casually mentioned that if one worker fell off. The family would get a few thousand pesos, and life would move on. The value of a life in Mexico is nothing compared to Canada. Another moment is captured in my picture called "chicken run." You can see a mound of chicken carcasses in the box of the pickup. A steam of blood could be seen coming from the tail gate.

Those chickens were going to be sold at a market! I lost my appetite for chicken for a while in Mexico City.

The most evident difference in dealing with a Mexican is how quickly and often the word Si Senor is used. These two words, of course, simply mean Yes, Sir. It was the way I was translating them for several weeks in the early days of my visits. However, as time went on, it became obvious that the words mean many other things. The meanings do not become clear until the situation arises; only then can one tell the difference.

To fully appreciate how the situations bring about the different meanings of Si Senor, it is best to take you through some of them. The meanings will vary from the simple literal translation to "I do not know," "I do not care," "None of your business," "Wouldn't you like to know," "I wish I knew," "get lost," "I understand," "Not in your life," "You stupid Gringo", "You will never get it."

The 10 km race – Si Senor, the course is very nice.

• Occasionally, I have an experience that will be remembered forever. These times are triggered by some unusual event that is so special, forcing my brain to put it in a fresh spot where it will be remembered for some time. This event happened on the morning of December 5, 2004. Jesus Moctezuma picked me up right on time in front of the Camino Real at 7:30 am. As we drove off, I remarked on how punctual he was. Jesus is a Chemical Engineer with a specialty for details and a part time runner when he can break away from his long hours at work. He is single and puts in easily 70 hours/week. We both agreed that runners are very punctual people. We were off to my first 10 km race in Mexico City. Jesus, this past week as a very nice gesture to show me the culture of Mexico on my first weekend stay over for my project work arranged it all. As we drove southbound down the Periferico, I was amazed at how light the traffic was. I guess Sunday morning is a good time to get around Mexico City, which is otherwise a zoo. We picked up

Arnulfo Contreras just before turning off the Periferico heading to Taluca. We were on our way to Desierto de los Leones. The name sounded neat, but I had no idea what I was headed for until I read the Spanish entry form and noticed that the starting elevation said 2994 meters. As I did the metric conversion in my head, it sunk in that I was going to run a 10 km race at about 9000 feet elevation. My home routes are at 500 feet elevation. The biggest hill is an abandoned land fill with trails.

• As we continued to climb up the winding road to the start line, I asked Jesus if the elevation was really 3000 meters. He said SI SENOR with a perplexed look. He was probably thinking that I must have known about the elevation. It had not sunk into my mind yet. We reached the start line, and I also noticed that the temperature had dropped from about 55 deg F to 35 deg F. The place was teaming with people. The huge pine trees and steep valley below provided a magnificent scene. I had never run a race this scenic. It was like nothing I had ever seen before at any race in Canada or USA. We got our running gear on and went for a short warm up run. The number of participants was almost 1000.

• The race start was on a flat spot on the road, but it quickly began a gradual rise. After about 2 minutes of running, I began to feel weak all over almost like wanting to fall asleep. A strange feeling. I thought it was probably from yesterday. I spent 5 hours walking around on a beautiful tour of downtown. I normally can take a hard day before a race, but this feeling was different. It would not go away. At the 1 km mark, I looked at my watch. It said 5:35; wow, I thought I normally do 4:30 on 10 km runs at home. OK, I said to myself, this is going to get better. At km 2, we were still climbing, my pace was not picking up but getting slower. It crossed my mind to start walking. Then I thought, no way I have run 9 marathons. I can do this race…I am not stopping. At about 2. 5 km, the course flattened out, but my pace did not pick up. Here I said OK, I am going to hang in there, but my breathing was so hard that it felt like I was running flat out. I had no legs at all. We continued flat, and at the 4 km mark, the lead runners passed me on their return leg. They zipped past me at lightning speed. They were doing 3 min/km; I was doing 5 min/km. The top 3 were Mexico, Mexico, and Kenya. I later checked their times, which were all just over 31 minutes for a 10 km race at 3000 meters!!! As I turned the 5 km loop, I passed Jesus, who was a few minutes back, then passed Arnulfo. On the way to the finish line, there was a bit of a climb followed by a nice slope all the way to the finish line. I crossed it at 53:31.

- This was a full 12 minutes slower than my personal best…Welcome to 3000 meters, Angelo!!! I waited for Jesus, who came in at 57 minutes, and Arnulfo at 1 hr 2 min. The finish line was full of cheering people. It was a great scene. A lifetime experience. The best part was getting a nice medal. We never get medals in short races back home. The restaurant was a very tiny, packed place that served the best fresh squeezed OJ with a Mexican Special breakfast (Potatoes, thin cuts of fried beef, melted cheese, greens that looked like beans but were not, and guacamole). The place was teeming with people, little kids, dogs, vendors, and colorful pottery…. unique. I got back to the Camino Real at noon. Laid down exhausted and woke up at 3:30 p.m. welcome to high elevation.

MEANING OF SI SENOR:

In this case, Jesus honestly believed that he was taking me to a typical race. Both of us failed to realize that we came from different elevations. It is a lesson in awareness of differences in our environments that are often taken for granted.

The Car accident – Si senor it will be repaired immediately

On a bright Sunday morning in early December, as we started a gradual climb we slowed down as the cars ahead did the same thing. We got closer to the slow down area and noticed that we were being veered to the right because an accident had happened just a few minutes before. A Green & White old VW taxi had been plowed into by what looked like Intrepid. I was looking ahead at the police and the accident, but at the corner of my left eye, I noticed the front end of a very large truck right on top of our car. I was just about to say something to Jesus but was interrupted by a crunching and rubbing sound. A stake truck that just continued to creep into us instead of stopping hit us. Jesus did all he could to keep to the right but could not react. We were seen by the police at the main accident and waved to the side. They never came over. As we stopped, Jesus and Arnulfo got out. I stayed in the car for just a few more seconds and noticed the truck beginning to roll back into us. We all started yelling, and miraculously, the truck driver stopped the truck just before he almost hit Jesus' car a second time!!!

One by one, four passengers got out of the truck. The driver had a baseball cap and ponytail. He was glossy eyed and incoherent, and drunken (7:50 a.m.). He looked like a double of the bad guys in the movie Man on Fire. I was standing there in my running shorts in amazement. Jesus was distraught. Arnulfo was in the back seat wide, wide-eyed, and perplexed. The second young man got out of the truck, stumbling. The third did the same thing. The fourth was so drunk that he needed to sleep on Jesus's hood. What a sight!!!

The conversation went on for quite some time. I felt so badly for Jesus. He was going to miss work to get his car fixed was having a heck of a time with the boys. The only this that was comforting was that there were 3 of us, and I think it helped protect Jesus. It may have been different if he was alone with 4 drunks. I had my DVD camera, so I continued to take pictures for evidence. Jesus was able to convince the drive to give up his insurance information. He called the insurance company on his cell and got an agreement that they did not have to come to the scene since the same company insured both parties. As we were ready to leave, the driver became upset. I thought that there were going to be fists flying, but his buddies managed to send him back to the truck. The two more sober friends seemed more cooperative. One of them came over and shook my hand as a friendly gesture. After about 25 min, we got back in the car. I asked if his car would be repaired, he said, "SI SENOR." we have the same insurance company, and it should be no problem. We drive off with a very nice gouge on the driver side rear door. Jesus went on to tell me that the drunken boys were heading to work. They were furniture movers!!!

MEANING OF SI SENOR:

What Jesus did not mention is that when a repair job is needed it can take months of red tape to complete it. He eventually got the car repaired in early May 2005, 6 months after the accident. It is common in everyday life to have to wait for months and hours of phone calls to get a service or repair done the normal way. There is, of course, the fast track that requires cash payments to a clerk or official along the way.

The Hotel Receptionist – The Graveyard Shift

I normally go out for a workout every morning at about 5:15 a.m. In Mexico this is a very early time. Most people stay out much later work nights. They also get going later in the morning. At the Crowne Plaza Hotel I had to go and ask the front desk attendant every morning to open the gym for me. One morning, I decided to have a bit of conversation with a young man who was looking a bit sleepy to get him energized.

As I was headed away from him to the gym, I casually said, "Too bad you are working the graveyard shift." He replied to SI SENOR. At this point, I realized that he had no idea what the meaning of "graveyard shift" was. I turned around and decided to help the young man. I asked him, "Do you know what graveyard means? He said, "No, senor". I realized that he had previously said yes but really meant no.

I proceeded to explain the meaning of graveyard to him. It was not easy. I described it by my broken translation of cemetery, dead people, quiet night, finally, his eyes lit up, and he understood the meaning. Next came the word shift. I asked him if he knew what the word "shift" meant. He picked up his computer keyboard and pointed to the "shift" key. I again used several descriptions of how schedules move around or "shift," at which point he again lit up, signaling that he had finally understood.

At the point of clearly understanding the full meaning, he thanked me and asked if I would write down the words. He mentioned that he planned to tell all his friends about the new words he had just learned.

MEANING OF SI SENOR:

The young hotel desk clerk works in the hospitality industry. He is programmed to always smile and use agreeable words. Even if he does not understand what you are saying, he will say yes, sir, because saying no is a negative sign and, in their view, shows disrespect.

The Political Rally – Si Senior, you can go through.

On a bright Saturday morning in April 2005, I was awakened by loud music playing at about 6:00 a.m. After looking down on to the street and calling the front desk, I was told that the hotel street intersection was going to be sued as the stage for a rally for the local region councillor who was coning in later that day. After listening to the loud Latino beat and the live band setting up. I went for my morning run and prepared to go out. When I again looked down on to the street, I noticed that the crowds were now moving in. It quickly dawned on me that I may not be able to get out with my car. I had plans to meet at the Museo Antropologico at 11:00 a.m.

I decided to leave quickly before the crowd blocked in the hotel garage. As I got the car from the parking attendant, I asked him are you sure I can get out with the crowds out there? He said, "SI SENOR."

As the nose of my VW Golf stuck out on to the street, I realized that it would be impossible for me to drive to an open street through the crowds. I have never been surrounded by a sea of people, alone and at the wheel of a car, and in a strange city. I had one of those moments of "I do not belong here." Backing up was too late; I could no longer see the hotel garage attendant or flag boy. I was alone creeping through ladies with buggies, men with young children, street vendors with carts full of big aluminum vats of something that was steaming. The looks on all their faces were not at all friendly. They looked surprised and at the edge of anger as if they were saying, "Get out of here," with their frowned faces. Not a good scene.

I finally made it to the open and squeezed through a barricade guarded by a Federale.

MEANING OF SI SENOR:

The hotel parking attendant, in this case, believed that he was sending me into a perfectly OK situation. In his view, there is nothing wrong with a car meandering through a street packed with pedestrians. My viewpoint, of course, was completely different.

The Soccer game – Si Senior, it will be easy to get there

Mexicans love their soccer. Every person at the plant has a favorite team. The factory soccer field has a game every Friday afternoon. Miguel, the taxi driver, knows every team in the Americas and Europe. Every night, the hotel satellite stations have about half a dozen games playing. Mexico City has 4 professional tier 1 teams.

The fans are wildly into their teams. Painted faces, flags, and smoke bombs are common scenes at every game. The plant queen of soccer mania is a young lady named Jessica. Her team is the famous UNAM Pumas. The Pumas are the equivalent of the Yankees of Mexico City. Pumas' fans are mostly young university kids since UNAM is one of the main universities.

On Wednesday evening, Jessica invited me to a Pumas game against rival Monterrey. Tom Bauer, who happened to be with me helping with logistics planning work, came along. Tom is in his early thirties and a tall ~200 lb American young man.

There we are off to the game. Jessica is the chauffeur. The game start time is at 8:30 p.m. As we headed out, the famous words came out when I asked if we would make it there for game time. SI SENOR said Jessica. It was 6:00 p.m., and we had to drive 50 km from the north end to the south end of Mexico City.

As we crawled along the Periferico highway, I was in the back seat, Tom in the front. Jessica is merrily chatting away, listening to Mexican music. At 8:00 p.m., the stadium is not yet visible. We drove along the section of Periferico that is being twinned. The new road is a massive structure suspended over the existing road. The earthquake pillars and the base of the road are a sight to be seen. The project has been going on for years and will last for another 10 years. The work is done with nightly closures, bringing traffic jams beyond imagination. As we headed south, we were not aware that the return trip had to be made that night.

We arrived at the game at 8:45. It took 2 ¾ hours from the time we left the plant. Jessica decided to show us where the action was. WE were in the student section. I realized by looking around that I was twice as old as the average crowd. Only one crowd control police looked close to 50 years old.

10 minutes after we got there, we had a Corona been cup in one hand and potato chips in the other that became our supper. We had not eaten a thing, thinking that we would grab something on the way. At that point, Jessica's friends arrived. Three couples, all from UNAM. A lawyer, a chemistry teacher, and a radio disk jockey were among them. We were all high spirited, laughing, giving high fives, and ready to party. In Mexico City, things are just getting going at

9:00 p.m. As we looked to our left, we noticed the standing crowd moving in a wave towards us. Jessica yelled out to move. Someone had released a smoke/tear bomb. As I began to run to my right, my throat was burning with a peppery taste. It was a bizarre moment as I hopped seats with my beer in one hand. As we did the shuffle to one side, Tom looked like he was having a blast.

After the smoke cleared, we went back to our spots, and I finally began to take in the game. The first half had just finished. UNAM was down 2-0. The young crowd was taking in the beer and getting restless. During halftime, the crowds never stopped hopping and singing their local chants. The crowd was the entertainment. We continued our beer and potato chips. Every time I looked around, one of Jessica's friends was putting a beer cup in my hand. At one time, I had 2 going. The potato chips were soaked with chili sauce just dumped into this big plastic bag that we were all grabbing from.

Just as we were grabbing chips from the communal bag, another rush of the crowds from my left began. This time, it was a fight in the flag waving seats that had caused people to flee from the center of the disturbance. The wave of people from below looked a bit like an ocean tide, innocent at first, then suddenly into where we were. That was when we all had to make a run for it one more time or be trampled.

As I continued to take in the whole scene of about 70,000 people on a warm Wednesday night at the Mexico City Olympic stadium, it dawned on me that this was a great exhibit of the love of life and fun Mexicans have, and we do not. By 9:30 p.m., most Canadians are already in bed, not out at a soccer game. The game ended 2-1 for the Monterrey team. As we were leaving it was now time to party for most of the crowds. Jessica asked us if we wanted to go out for supper. It was almost 11:00 p.m. I gracefully declined, although young Tom might have wanted to go along. The reason why I declined was because I suddenly realized that we had a two-hour ride back and an early meeting the next day.

Jessica went into action and took us to her favourite taxi pick up area. She stated that these guys were trustworthy and reliable and guaranteed to get us back to the Crowne Plaza. As we approached the classic old VW bug green and white taxi, I began to think trouble was ahead. This was only because of the many stories I have heard about taxi drivers robbing foreigners, beat ups, etc. Tom was also looking a bit skeptical about the whole thing. After a few minutes of negotiations, Jessica paid the driver and told us the next stop would be the hotel. We got into the back through the missing front seat. That is the way the standard VW taxi is equipped. Tom to my left, and off we went. With the two of us in the little vehicle, the suspension system was leaning to the left as we moved down the street.

After a few minutes of slow-moving turns, I realized that we were not headed back to the Periferico main highway but were on side streets with wall-to-wall traffic. It was almost 11:30 by this time, and I was looking at Tom, who was also apprehensive about the whole situation. It was the first time that I felt a bit out of place, and it crossed my mind that if something nasty happened I had a big guardian angel with me. It was then that my cell phone rang, and it was Jessica. She wanted to know if we were OK. I told her that we were surprised to be in such heavy traffic that late at night. I knew that things were bad in the south end of the city, but I did not think that it would be that bad. That is when she finally clarified what happens every night in the south end. The main road is closed, so they continue to build the suspended new highway. Surprise, I guess I should have realized that on the way in, but I didn't.

The taxi driver finally merged onto the Periferico at about 12:30 a.m. Jessica called again. I told her that we were now in the clear. It was very nice to hear from her. It felt like getting calls from my worried mom or wife. From that point on, we only hit one more spot where the road was detoured, this time because of road painters. We were in bed by about 1:00 a.m.

MEANING OF SI SENOR –

Jessica's intentions when she said we would get to the game on time were truthful and honest. Getting to the game almost halfway through the first half is not uncommon. As a matter of fact, getting anywhere late is the rule, not the exception. We do not see it that way because we all show up on time. WE do not have to fight through the stifling traffic of a city that stretches 100 km and has 25 million people. It is like all of Canada living in Essex County.

Paris

You've heard a few travel stories and here's another one that is quite pleasant. It happened just before I turned 40. While traveling between Toronto and Windsor on a Dash 8 an early morning at a 7 am flight, a draw that if you got your seat number drawn you won a prize from Air Canada. For some lucky reason, I ended up getting two tickets to anywhere in the world first class that Air Canada flies. I went home, and the only thing that came to mind between Rosella and me was that we needed to go to Paris. The trip was one of the best experiences that happened during my BASF tenure, and that required every ounce of energy from me. We went without knowing what all happening in France; we took three thousand dollars this is mid '90s, thinking that this would be enough for our 10 days; on the fourth day, I ended up going to Paris Bank and drew another five thousand dollars; long story short it was very expensive but fun like crazy the best part was us flying first class it was wonderful.

Some of the highlights that we picked up in France were one, please don't drive in Paris, so after a couple of days, I returned the rent-a-car, and we took transportation the TV that went to the south of France was an excellent experience, and there we experienced all of the wonderful things of Monaco, Le Côte d'Azur, Nice, and traveled back up into Paris.

Some of the highlights that also took place during that time were the incredible prices that would happen for tourists. One was we needed to see Notre Dame Cathedral up close, so we went to a bar and ordered a cappuccino with a sweet and when it was brought to us and the bill came, I noticed that it was outrageously priced. I asked why, and we were told that because we were sitting in the viewing area of the restaurant, it was three times the price. It's one of those things that stay with you, and I thought maybe we could have just sat in a regular seat, but it was worth every minute. And the entire price was worth it. So, it's just a wonderful experience that we shared, and a highlight was on my 40th birthday; I was sitting in front of the Louvre, reading a newspaper, the Figaro, and it's a site. I still have a picture that I'll remember forever, and we had more baguettes and more croissants than you can imagine. Seeing the sights of France, it's an experience of a lifetime.

European Experience

I had an interesting experience during my travels with BASF. And it involved us going for vendor visits to buy a piece of equipment that is an automated paint dispenser. We call it the Coke machine. You go up and get your color. We went to three different companies to get the same equipment specified and described and finalize the purchase. First, we went to a German company. The German company was very, very precise. They toured us. They gave us a beautiful presentation with all the technical information. However, there was just one small problem. The price was way, way over what we had budgeted. As we were leaving, we were told, this is what you must have, and this is the price. We can't change it, to which we said, sorry, but we're going to have to think about this. It's way, way too much. It was almost twice what we had in mind.

As we were leaving, I happened to mention that we were going to an Italian company near Milan. The look on their faces was one of stunned looks because one of them said, "You cannot compare us to the Italians." The Italians have inferior technology. They only do shiny things. However, their quality is not like ours. As we arrived to meet the Italian company, the Dromont president met with me, gave me a hug, and we got treated like royalty. We spent most of the morning having sweets and espresso. The whole time my partners were asking where all the technical information is. We spent almost the entire day schmoozing, but we didn't really get to see the machine until the early afternoon. As we walked through the plant, the only thing that we got from their lead engineer was, "It looks sexy." It's one line that I will not forget; of course, the German engineer looked at me and shook his head. As we left, we told them that we were going to a British company near London. The Italians did a similar thing as in Germany; they said, "How dare you go off the European continent? The British are not us; they are not very precise, and you must buy from us". As we left, the president gave me that Italian handshake and said to Angelo, "You're my paisano, and you have to buy from us." Off we went to England. The British were formal, the dinner was precise, we were on time the dispensing machine parts were all beautiful. We had a great visit; everything was laid out with precision; of course, we got the lecture that

Canadians can only buy from the British because they're still using the British system, and we are the ones who must buy from them because the Europeans are substandard and they're on the metric system. As we left that visit three of us got so much different information. It was amazing, and when it was all over and done, we ended up buying from another company in Holland. There's a little story about Europe and how different each culture is. One day, in a discussion with Dr. Hans Reichart, I got an awakening. He went on to tell me that he could not figure me out. You are an Italian living in Canada with an engineering degree. He continued to explain that Italians are known for food and sex. He could not understand how an engineer fit into that view of life that he has.

Business Travels

My business trips to Alabama were always full of surprises because the weather was very unpredictable, especially in the summertime. One Friday, when I was coming back to Detroit from Huntsville, I was notified that there was a thunderstorm coming and tornadoes possibly. The weather delay took place, and I was lucky enough to get the last flight, not to Detroit, but through Chicago with American Airlines. I left at around 4 o'clock and by the time I crossed over from Chicago to Detroit, I got to Detroit at around 1 a.m. At 1 a.m., all the transit buses had stopped. And that day I parked over at the Blue Deck, which is about half a mile from McNamara Terminal. What ended up happening was that I decided to walk from the terminal over to the parking lot and it was a long walk. I was tired. On the way over, the bus driver who was going to pick me up asked me if I wanted to ride. I said no. I kept going. I could see the Blue Deck. I could see the lighted parking decks. I decided to hop over the side of a ramp on the road and ran across the parking lot. When I got to the parkade, I noticed that there was a fence, so I climbed over it, threw my bags over, and on my way up, security came by. They looked at me and said, "Sir, what are you doing"? I said, "I'm tired. I'm late. I must get to my car". They looked the other way and kept driving. I got to the parkade. By this time, I was exhausted from carrying my bags. And lo and behold, I forgot which deck I was on. So, I walked back and forth, holding my key fob. I pushed the panic button, hoping that I could hear the car, and I finally heard it. By the time I was in the car, it was one of those days where I thought, oh my god, I made it. By the time I got home that night, it was about 2.30 in the morning, one of the longest and most weird flights that I've done back to get home.

Traveling out of Germany to different airports is also quite an interesting experience. The one time that I was flying, part business and part pleasure, I flew from Frankfurt to Madrid to Rome to see my relatives. The flight into Frankfurt was late from Dresden. When we got to Frankfurt, we were able to sleep overnight and get the flight to Madrid the next day. What ended up happening was that my luggage got mixed up, so when I got to Madrid, I had no luggage. I just had my carry-on, a little tiny bag. It was in the middle of summer, late August, and I was planning to go to Italy to see my relatives. Long story short, I ended up in Rome with a bag that had sandals, what I was wearing, and that was it. At Madrid airport, it took a while for us to see if we could find my luggage, which I couldn't. My most memorable experience was they took me to the lost luggage room. It was the size of a small gymnasium. And I told the attendant that I was looking for a Samsonite, the clothes one, the fold-over one. Well, when they took me to the section that had the Samsonites, it had to be like 150. And the short answer was I could not find my bag. I ended up going in shorts in August to my relatives. I spent the weekend there, and my luggage finally showed up the following week at home. All I can remember is my aunt washing my shorts and my top repeatedly because that's all I had for the whole weekend. But the best part was going into the lost luggage, which I'd never been to, and found that Samsonite with the carry-ons, there are so many, that it was just incredible to see a room full of all those black bags.

Mexico, Here We Come.

One more memorable assignment with BASF was in Mexico to transfer a product line from the USA. I will call this "The Missing Meter – Si senior, the meter will be there." As part of my role on the project it was my job to make sure that the details were looked after. The details are what make or make projects. Specifically, with the cultural differences, it is very important to stay on top of things. My role was often one of being able to read the situation with almost a sixth sense. That is when one must think through the possibilities, visualize all the possible things that could go wrong, and then follow up on the existing plans to make sure all systems are going.

We decided very early as a strategy that we would select the nastiest product on the transfer list, and it would be first up. The product on all counts, is very sensitive to process conditions and has a long history of being very unpredictable even after it has been verified that processing conditions are all ok.

One critical parameter identified to us very early was the requirement to measure the processing flow rate. We included the purchase of a new meter for this reason. As it neared the time to run the first batch, I decided to take a walk to the plant to check out the famous meter that I was promised, "Si Senor," it will be ready. As I made my way to the equipment, I noticed that the meter was not visible. Thinking that it was in a different spot than I usually would expect it, I asked the floor supervisor about the meter. The supervisor, in turn, replied, "Oh no, it is not here yet. It will be here in 2 to 3 weeks...." I was momentarily set back since we were expecting to run the product in about 10 days.

I followed up with the project manager and confirmed that the meter was really coming in after the first product run. At this point, I realized that we had to change our plans. Here I was with plans to have 3 Americans coming down to witness the first run product, and they would not see what was considered by them one of the most important measurements they expected.

During this time, my contact was away on vacation. I quickly requested that a used meter be provided, and it was quickly located. When my contact got back, it was obvious that he was not pleased with my intervention. The basic reason was that he believed that I was making a "big" deal of the fact that we were missing a "simple" meter. His plan was to use a manual valve to throttle the process fluid for control. I proceeded to explain that it would not be acceptable to improvise in such a manner. His reply was one of not understanding, and to this day, he still believes that his plan would have been just fine.

MEANING OF SI SENOR – In this case there was an honest belief that improvising would be just fine. Further, it was not understood that there are times when this is OK and others when it is not. To the credit of Mexican people, they are by far the best improvisers I have ever seen. The odd thing is that to us, they do look like sheer chaos. However, they do get the job done! We just must look the other way. Looking the other way for Gringos is often not an easy thing to do. I was able to deal with the Latin way of life with my Italian upbringing.

As time went on with plant closures and product transfers, my attitude began to decay, and so did my work quality.

At BASF, I spent 16 years with that great company. The start was rock with the Cornwall closure but eventually Windsor came along. The paint plant I built is still there today, and when I drive by it, memories come back from this tangible contribution to mankind. The new plant I built was used to produce materials from plant closures in the Detroit area. The business gains from the closures were so profitable that I got a job continuing the same model. What ended up happening at the very tail end of the title of rationalization manager really got to me. I was doing a terrible job meeting with plant managers and telling them that we were going to close them. I recall meeting one plant manager at the airport in Chicago. He knew what my job was; he did not want me to go to his plant because he knew that his plant was on the list to be either closed or sold. As we talked, he told me that he had been there for over 30 years and broke down in tears. The job eventually got to me to the point when lost my appetite to continue. I became cynical and began making mistakes at a job that required a delicate balance of business as well as compassion. The air miles and all the travel that I was doing lost its glamour.

On September 2, 2005, at 8:00 am, I met with John Sullivan and Scott Elliot. The meeting was confrontational and aimed solely at getting me to admit that the Greenville project overrun and engineering policies not followed were my fault. I left the meeting with no handshake and a curt goodbye from John Sullivan, who had the look of having me mentally already terminated. There was nothing amicable about the meeting, including the opening stern warning that this was a serious matter with serious possible consequences. As I left the meeting, I saw Sam Black at the corner of my eye in the Southfield lobby waiting area. He was obviously next up.

I went back to my office in Windsor with an ugly feeling that my career at BASF was over. Over the weekend, I thought about what had taken place and wrote the following. I got no reply from either Sullivan or Elliot. At the close of the interview, I was requested to provide any additional thoughts. At that point, I gave none but, at the same time, realized that the interview had turned from a clarification session to accusations of "poor judgment."

On Monday, September 12th, I received a request from Scott Elliott to "be in Windsor at 2:00 p.m. Sept 15th. I knew then that it would be my last day at BASF. The thought stayed with me for the whole time I visited Greenville for my weekly visit. The visit was bizarre because the whole time I did not get the ugly thought out of my mind. At exactly 2:00 p.m., Scott Elliott, Dave Buford, and Rita Rosato headed for my office in Windsor. The operators were moving about as shift change neared. Elliott sat and, in a monotone, almost tearful voice, stated, "…. Angelo, as you know, the Greenville overrun found through the recent audit that several engineering procedures were not followed. It is for this reason that BASF has decided to terminate your employment…" He then started to get up. I asked if I could say something. I had a note handwritten with the following statement "It is with deep regret that I leave BASF under such conditions. I truly believe that during my employment, I gave it all I had. However, it appears that it did not meet the high standards of BASF. I thank BASF for giving me 16 years of employment…"

I was then presented with a severance letter with 16 weeks' pay and a statement from the HR VP that it was a starting point, given the fact that while in the USA, I was not owed anything. He gave me some niceties and left. Rosato then cleaned up my items; I gave my BASF badge, Amex, and PC and drove off-site while watched by all the shift workers. That was the end of my BASF tenure. I decided to go and get my plate stickers on the way home. It was just another day. After I got home it started sinking in that it was for real. The evening of Sept 15th was a bit sad in the household. Rosella and Daniel were very supportive.

My departure from BASF was likely due to another moment where my attitude and inability to deal with acceptance of failure could have been a lot different. It was during my work transferring products from the US to Mexico. We hit a very difficult time, that was causing delays. I recall exactly when it happened. I was at Detroit airport on the overpass that goes from the terminal to the parking. I made a call to the director of logistics. The call was to explain to Jim that we were behind schedule. The reason was that the customer service team was having a very difficult time completing the product templates from English to Spanish. The conversation got very heated; I was tired since I had just landed from being in Mexico City for the week. I've been traveling a lot. The product transfers are very late, and for some reason, I cannot explain why I use the f word for the director of logistics who was on the phone. The conversation ended, and we said goodbye. It was over the weekend. Monday morning, I got a call from my Scott Elliot, who asked what happened. I explained it, and all I remember hearing from Scott was, "Angelo, it's not a good idea to use the f word with the director of logistics." The rest unfolded with BASF. Looking back at the job I was doing and the away time from Daniel and Rosella. It was the best thing that happened to me in 2005.

That same night, I got busy on the e mails looking for employment. Sept 16th – Got names of lawyers to go after BASF for more money. David McNiven was my selection. Sept 18th was my annual ½ marathon at Point Pelee. It was a hotter than usual day, but I still did 1:38 and was second in the age group.

These are diary entries: Sept 19th – Visited Lawyer McNiven and decided to ask for 18 months with a reasonable expectation to get at least 8 months. Sept 22nd – Contacted Tech Hi, who mentioned that Commercial Alcohols had a position open. Sept. 26th – I Interviewed with Marty Cormier and Katie Kelley. The interview went well, and I got a good feeling that I was on my way to a new position. Sept 28th – I had a second interview and received a job offer for Eng & Maintenance Manager. October 1 accepted position to start Oct 11th. October 5[th,] BASF offers 8 months' severance, and I accept.

CHAPTER 7

A Eulogy

Chris Stanford is one of the most memorable and admirable people of my life. Here are my thoughts to honour his life.

A Tribute to Chris Stanford

July 3, 2015

It is with a bruised heart that I stand here today, representing the place and people that Chris changed forever. We have all gotten to know Chris very well indeed, whether it was from the very early days in Tiverton doing summer work with his dad Mike, the

Chris was the Operator on shift, the Operations Manager, and the Maintenance Manager at the Chatham plant. Chris was not only our colleague but our friend. He taught us many things, but most importantly, he showed us how to live life, fight for what you believe in, and have strength and courage in all that you do. Chris redefined how to conquer fear like no one could. I can do that. Leave it with me. I'll take care of it. This is the plan…. are the only phrases that Chris knew. In 2001 the Tiverton wastewater lagoon pump was not pumping. Chris said I can fix that. Helped by another, he went in headfirst, reaching deep below the water while held by his feet. The pump began to work again. In 1997, Chris was given all the operating manuals by Flour Daniel and was told this is how you run Chatham. He did that. In 2008, I asked Chris to run the operations department. He said you can count on me to do that, and I want to take the Dale Carnegie course so I can speak fancy just like you. He took care of that. In December 2013, Chris came to me and said I want to get a business degree because someday I want to do your job…I said, Chris……I am sure you can do that…..On January 29, 2014, Chris came to me and said I have this setback in me that I need to get fixed. I will be back in the fall, and once it's all better, I still want to get my business diploma. On May 29, 2014, after losing a friend to cancer, Chris wrote "…. For Ray and all the others who are faced with such extreme cases, I ask that if you have not already donated to a Relay for Life participant, you please consider doing so. Every dollar puts us that closer to a cure, and without a cure, we will all be touched by this nasty disease in one shape or form over

Our lifetime….". The Greenfield Relay for Life team set a fund-raising record in 2014.

On June 15, 2015, Chris waved me in after the 5km run at Trot to the Beach. He said you must have a beer with me. I was tired; it was 9:30 in the morning, and my first thought was…that beer would really do me in…. instead, I said I can do that! I will remember that beer forever. While fighting cancer, Chris became the hero to so many because he put our own minuscule daily struggles in a perspective that we have never experienced.

Chris Stanford set the bar very high for us. The word "fighter" has a new meaning....

How is it that an Italian immigrant lady just 4 feet 11 inches has so much impact on so many?

I will try my best to use the words that she taught me because I am a continuation of her spirit on this earth. I stand here today to tell everyone how her love and relentless positive energy brought us together. I also hope to live up to her dream of a Padre Angelo. My Franciscan seminary career was cut short because I was a bit of a rebel like her. So how is it that I can express the full sentiment of Caterina, the excellent mother, wife, sister, cook, ambassador of goodwill, nurse to many, teacher, and political analyst?

One of my sisters told me that mom always wanted to be a boy. She felt that my experiences were hers. She once dressed up at Carnival back in Italy so that she could get drunk while the other girls sat nicely, waiting to be asked to dance. The next day, she woke up with a big headache in a field and said, "Ah, this is what it's like to be a boy," so the story goes.

Mom is the one who exemplified the values of Honesty, Integrity, Respect, Commitment, and Openness to Change. What do these words mean? It's best to describe how mom defined them for us.

Honesty....that means say what you mean and mean what you say.....there I was at Woolworths shopping for high school clothes with mom...Fred, the Men's department head, just packed the clothes, and Mom opened the bag to check them...by the way, Fred is 6 feet tall and towered over Mom...She looks at him and says, " I want 25% off these Jeans because they have a frayed spot, and besides... How dare you try to take me for a fool after all these years I come here to buy clothes from you? "I have never seen a big man like that wilt like a flower and apologize several times she got her 25% off. Of course, I was embarrassed, but I did not know that she just taught me about honesty and to speak your mind.

Integrity is a big and adult word that, even today I don't understand. Mom lived, talked, expressed, and repeatedly was so predicable in her love of her family and everyone she touched. Her endless desire to look way past the pettiness of life was uncanny. She often had thoughts that were insightful and timed at times in our lives that made tremendous changes happen for the better. It's only a person who is viewed by others with the highest integrity that can change relationships and people's lives significantly. Caterina's Integrity was immense.

What can I say about commitment and our mom, Caterina? She dedicated every essence of her life to raising her kids and helping our dad, Giovanni, with immeasurable and exemplary passion. Her devotion to her dad was over 75 years strong. Her commitment to us paid dividends for her. How is it that I can say that...? Many times, I would show up with Anna, Toni, and Stefania at a function, doctor's office, or other occasions, and I would hear comments like..." It's hard to believe that the 4 of you are so well harmonized and know your place, especially at these times when tough decisions need to be made...." It all happened because Caterina's kids were taught all about commitment by watching her live her life.

As for respect, she earned it by promoting harmony and always finding the best in her family and those that she touched. Here is a passage from her many journals notes about how she saw her kids and earned respect from all of us." You never know how much you mean to me. You always come home on every occasion. Getting together is very important not just for the food but for the love of family. Angelo, you are older and very understanding, and I appreciate it. You and Anna make everything easy. Toni and Stefania follow you nicely. Today Dad and I went shopping and spent the money that you gave us...."

Mom Caterina

One more example of how Mom earned respect is best described by my dear lifetime friend from LDSS, Paul Taylor.

"Dear Angelo, it is with such heavy hearts that we send you this message after learning of the passing of your mom. There are many things that we reminisce about when someone we love is no longer with us....with respect to your mom; it was always her sweet smile, the loving way she pronounced your name, asking if you wanted her to make pizza for the guys after we had been out for the evening and of course the care package of Ciammelle that regularly arrived in London...." Mom was the provider of food and love for my best friends Paul Taylor, Kirk James, Dave Tippett, Rick Gulliver, Herb Kreling, and Jim Hillier. They ended up falling in love with her cooking and thought they liked Mom more than they liked me. They smile every time her name comes up.

Meeting Mr. Brown again

I met Mr. Brown's wife, Mary, at Mom's funeral. She mentioned that Mom always talked to her about me but had not seen me in over 40 years. I asked Mary if I could reconnect with Mr. Brown…here are the notes we wrote.

Dear Bill:

It's been nearly 50 years since we crossed paths. This past Wednesday night, I met your wife, Mary, at mom's funeral visitations. As we talked, we began reminiscing about my days at Queen of Peace. I told her my story about the time I was suspended for my misbehavior.

The irony of this story is the fact that after you suspended me, I told my mom that I was sent home for being so smart. We had only been in Canada for 3 years, so she spoke little English and read even less. At that time mom believed me as any mother would. However, during that summer, before I headed to high school, I had to do a lot of soul searching. She did eventually find out as all mothers do.

Respectfully…. Angelo

Mr. Brown replies….

Hi Angelo,

Thanks for the note and for sharing the story that goes with it. While we haven't had direct contact over all these years, your dad always kept us up to date when we would see him during our visits to Maria's mom. He would usually stop in, and we would get to catch up on you and your siblings - if anything was obvious, it was simply that your dad loved all of you very much, and he was proud of his children - as he should be!

I do remember the story you shared but not all the details around it. It was interesting for me to read my own letter to your parents - sorry for being so nasty at the time. I always look back at my years at Queen of Peace as some of the best years of my life. It's not that I haven't had many good years; it's just putting them in the perspective of a lifetime.

Maybe what you wouldn't be aware of was my lack of experience and maturity at the time. There are many things I did in my younger years that I would do differently now. It is amazing how our outlooks change as we gain experience, meet others, and gain perspective. I do remember that, at the time, since there were only a few days left in the year, a suspension would not have any impact on your studies, and I knew you were going to graduate anyway (you were a bright student). For me, it was a way to try to bring a young student face to face with responsibility.

You always reminded me of myself when I was in elementary snchool. I was always in one escapade or another, and I, too, had some fantastic teachers along the way who made such a difference to me. One of them was my elementary school principal. She was a sister of St Joseph who now lives in London at her mother's house there and is over 90 years old. We visit her on occasion and have a delightful time-sharing story about my misdemeanors. In the mists of time, we can laugh about them now as we share them from each other's perspective - me as a mischievous child and her working at helping me through my experiences.

I am so pleased to hear from you and what happened after you left elementary school. I was not aware of some of your accomplishments so belated congratulations! Bill

Caterina Scholarship

In honor of mom, Caterina, who always wanted to be a boy. And she told me later in life that she lived her life watching me going through engineering. In 2019, we set up a fund that reads as follows.

The Caterina Ligori Engineering Award is awarded annually to a full-time undergraduate female student in year two or higher in the Faculty of Engineering at UWO who has achieved a minimum of 75% average in the previous year and has shown exemplary support and encouragement to others through participation in extracurricular activities and mentorship. Applicants must complete by September 30 the engineering undergraduate website outlining how they have demonstrated their support and encouragement for others in the spirit of life values that Caterina lived by. Preference will be given to a female student whose parents immigrated to Canada. The undergraduate awards committee in the Faculty of Engineering will select the recipient. This award was established as a generous gift from Angelo Ligori, Bachelor of Engineering Science, 1978, and his wife, Rosella, in memory of his mother; Caterina raised four children following the values of integrity, honesty, respect, commitment, and openness to change. With only grade three formal schooling, Caterina used these life values to empower all her children to grow. The Scholarship value is $1,000 every year.

CHAPTER 8

What is Wisdom?

The polar vortex experience defined courage for me and all Chatham Greenfield team.

1. On January 6, 2014, Chatham experienced a once every 60-year cold snap that was named Polar Vortex.

2. The temperature dropped unusually fast from -10 deg C to -27 deg C between 12 noon and 8 p.m. Wind chills were recorded at -43 deg C.

3. By 8 am, I was informed that the Technical Manager, Process Engineer and Engineering Manager were snowed in and would work from home.

4. I was late due to heavy drift in the driveway that had to be cleared, restart of the home furnace due to blocked exhaust, and attempted restart of a hot water heater.

5.   The morning got off to a slow start due to several other employees being snowed in. The cause was heavy wind gusts to 50 km/hr. That started overnight and continued all day. I was called home to clear the furnace exhaust a second time.

6.   During the morning, plant operations continued as normal, and preparations were made to bring in extra people for the oncoming cold night.

7.   At 1:55 pm, with ambient temperatures around -17 degrees C and wind chills of -30 degrees C, an instrument failed due to freezing.

8.   The instrument failure eventually made the boilers fail.

9.   At 2:04, the air compressors tripped. Within 14 minutes, there was a sequential loss of cooling water, instrument air that controls the entire plant, and steam for the entire plant.

10. The plant was frozen for one week, causing losses of about $1 Million, but everyone was safe.

The Chatham Ethanol Plant is the flagship of Greenfield Global. I am proud to have had the opportunity to be the Plant Manager for 10 years.

The Greenfield Global Chatham Ethanol Plant is my proudest career moment. I wrote the article that appears below as proof of my life philosophy to Mother Earth.

2012 - Angelo Ligori: Sensible, renewable ethanol Angelo Ligori, Special to National Post | Sep 18, 2012, 5:39 PM ET

Fuel ethanol has been a popular media subject this summer. Is it really because of a record drought in the Midwest U.S.? I am the manager of one of Canada's largest ethanol plants in Chatham, Ont., and have lived both the science and economics of ethanol production for over 15 years. It continues to amaze me how the media, and through it, the Canadian public, has been hoodwinked about ethanol.

There is much at stake here. Powerful vested interests see ethanol as a threat. Big Oil has enjoyed a monopoly on your gas tank for almost a century. For decades, cattle and hog producers have benefited from cheap corn because of billions of dollars in government agricultural subsidies. But over the last 10 years, governments of all stripes around the world have legislated renewable fuel mandates. As a result, grain ethanol is now 10% of the gasoline pool in North America. That's about 14 billion gallons or 50 billion liters of ethanol production. It's a huge change; and it's natural to expect that certain sectors of the economy would want to reverse this and return to the old status quo.

So, they are now waging a war to influence public opinion to intimidate the government to remove the ethanol mandate. It's not going to happen. Ethanol opponents have been using the opportunity of a 50-year drought to crank up the hysterics. But the truth is governments have embraced ethanol because the facts show it is overwhelmingly sensible to do so. It helps to clean up tailpipe emissions, generates real greenhouse gas reductions, reduces our dependence on foreign oil, provides jobs and stimulates incredible economic activity in rural communities.

Here are a few published, peer-reviewed facts about ethanol that have been misrepresented in this summer's media reports:

• Only 1% of corn grown in North America is for human consumption at the dinner table. The rest is industrial or feed corn.

• Only the carbohydrate from the industrial (not food) grade corn is used to make ethanol. 100% of the protein, fiber, minerals, vitamins, and oils are returned to the animal feed market in the form of distillers' grains.

• The United Nations Food and Agriculture Organization says that there is enough food produced annually to feed everyone on Earth. Hunger in the third world results from political strife, corruption and failures of food distribution — not from ethanol production.

• The amount of industrial corn used for North American ethanol production last year is roughly equal to the increase in the annual corn crop over the past 10 years, driven by advances in agricultural practices and seed genetics. Corn demand for ethanol has been the catalyst for these advancements.

• Even at today's high corn prices, ethanol is cheaper than gasoline on a mileage-equivalent basis. A 2011 study conducted by researchers at the University of Iowa concluded that without ethanol, the average pump price of gasoline would have been over $1 per gallon higher.

• The real driver of food inflation is energy costs for transportation, storage, and marketing. A farmer only gets 14.1¢ of the store price, whereas marketing, labor, packaging, transportation, storage, and processing costs are 84.9¢.

• Ethanol is a safe, natural alternative to the aromatics traditionally used for octane enhancement, and which have been linked to emissions of ultra-fine particulates that cause asthma and other respiratory ailments.

• Ethanol is also an oxygenate, which means that its inclusion in gasoline promotes a more complete combustion with fewer tailpipe emissions. That's one of the reasons why NASCAR and the Indy cars run on ethanol — it's more powerful because of the octane, and the cleaner exhaust is easier on the spectators.

• Grain ethanol produced at modern ethanol plants generates greenhouse gas reductions of about 60% relative to conventional gasoline. This is important because 30% of Canada's greenhouse gas emissions come from the transportation sector.

• The energy balance of ethanol is very good and getting better all the time. You get between 1.6 and two units of energy output for every unit of energy input.

Meanwhile, I have seen the future. We are making next generation advanced biofuels in Chatham from agricultural waste like corn cobs and stover, from energy crops like switch grass and tall prairie grass, and from wood waste, including sawdust and wood chips. Canadians should be proud of our engineers and scientists as we pioneer the development of advanced biofuels. I am fully committed to our industry. I love my job and have seen firsthand that ethanol has created skilled jobs at the plants, work for truckers, grain elevator operators, and so much more for the community of Chatham, which was hard hit by lay-offs and plant closures. All motorists should feel good knowing that 10% of what's in their gas tank is ethanol — the sensible local clean-burning renewable fuel. Don't be fooled into thinking otherwise.

LEADERSHIP

My personal and professional leadership traits are below. Many of them I learned and practiced at Greenfield Global. They come from observing others that I admire. The traits are often a reminder for me when I drift, of course.

1. Acts, not react.

2. Knows why, not how.

3. Do not blame others.

4. Learned from experience.

5. Resolves conflict with grace,

6. Coaches people to succeed.

7.   Organizes and communicates.

8.   Is dependable and persistent.

9.   Has a natural affinity for people.

10. Focuses on values and aspirations.

11. Is a problem finder, not a problem solver?

12. Has intuition to prioritize complex situations.

13. Has a vision that is simple, desirable, and energizing.

14. Reinforces long range thinking, innovation, and creativity.

15. Sees that the right work, not lots of work, gets done.

16. Can explain complex plans so that they are easy to follow.

Vegas

In December 2018, I was sent to Las Vegas on a special project I was working on for the cannabis industry. When I got to the convention, it was a three-day convention. At the convention center in Vegas, it is unbelievably large. It just goes on and on and on. I had some fun there. Of course, I was one of the elders because the cannabis generation that was there was in their 20s and 30s, and I'm in my late 60s, so it was quite a sight to see the young crowd and the look that they gave me.

The best part of my trip, though, was I ended up trying out one of the cannabis stores that was there. When I walked in, I was greeted by a big Samoan security guard who asked for my identification and whether it was for medicinal or pleasure. I went in. I finally selected some gummies, working with a young lady. I took gummies, and some were heavy on THC. I think one gummy was 9 milligrams, and the other one was CBD. While I was waiting to go to a Cirque du Soleil show, I decided to have a gummy. I had one of the THC ones. I almost took two because it took a long time for it to take effect, but by the time I had waited about an hour and a half and started walking to the show, I felt this euphoric feeling that made me feel like I was walking so fast, passing people and the trees going by me were slowly, slowly moving. There was a weird, weird feeling that I'd never had. Of course, the best part when I got there was watching Cirque du Soleil. Now, when you're watching Cirque du Soleil with all those actions and lights, and you are on THC, which I'd never been to, it was quite an experience. At one part, I thought I could go into the act and fly around like the people who were doing all the crazy moves on these trapezes. So, that was probably the highlight of my trip. But the first and only time that I took the THC gummies, I can tell you that it's quite an experience. After that, I decided it was not for me, but I just thought I would share that with you guys.

I just need to back up a bit from my THC gummies purchase in Las Vegas. When I went to make the purchase, I tried to use my visa, only to find out that it was missing from my wallet. I panicked and then realized that I had given it to a locksmith named Roman. So let me back up further. Roman came into my life that morning because when I went to the rent-a-car, I found that I couldn't get into it because it was locked. I called Hertz. I was trying to figure out how to unlock it, and they told me that the only way they could do it was they have a tow truck brought over, and it would cost over $350 to do that. They suggested that maybe I call a locksmith, which I did. I looked through Google to search for a locksmith. I found one, and he said that he was nearby. This was very early. It was about 8.30 on Friday morning, and what I did then, I waited for them. He came by at around 10.30, so I had to wait a long time. During that time, I discovered that I was able to get into the car through the trunk. And when I did that, I went through, I opened the trunk, I flipped the back seat down, and I got into the car. And while I was in the car, a couple of youngsters that were going to the casino looked in and asked if I was okay. I said everything was fine. I'm sure they went back home and said, "you wouldn't believe what I saw, an older guy crawling around through a car, and he said that everything was okay". Roman finally showed up. He was able to convince me that the key, the key fob, was somewhere near the car. After several tries, we discovered that I had it in my back pocket between the outside and my wallet. It's a very thin key fob. We got into the car. As I tried to pay him, I looked inside his vehicle, and it was full of all kinds of things, tools that he's using for locksmiths. And in a hurry, he swiped my card and took off. Lo and behold, I realized when I was at the cannabis store that Roman had taken my card with him. He came back hours later to give me my card so that I could then make the purchase. So that is now a connection between the THC story and Roman, the locksmith in Vegas.

41 Years Later January 21, 2024

In 1983 we visited Vegas but did not go to the Grand Canyon. Life happened after that; Rosella has always wanted to go back to see it. 40 years later, I finally booked the tickets to Vegas with Delta, leaving on January 16th and returning on January 19th. The plan was to use the 16th and 19th as travel days. One day at Zion National Park and one day at Grand Canyon Sky Walk. The Vegas stay was at the Bellagio because Rosella heard about it in Oceans 11. Here is another diary entry.

Tuesday, January 16, 2024.

We left at 9:30 for a 1:00 p.m. flight out of Detroit. Not far down the 401, we hit several accidents of jack-knifed trucks on black ice. My favorite was the red Jeep hanging on the guardrail. It was one of the colder nights at minus 15 C, and roads were not yet salted. Accidents we just happening, and we drove by some that we watched cars hitting the ditch to my right and the median wall to my left.

At 10:30 am, while on Southfield overpass 2nd lane from the right. I'm doing 100 km/h in Q7. The planes landing at the airport were visible straight ahead. On the lane to my left is a white F150 ahead of me, 3 car lengths. There are no vehicles in the other lanes next to us and F150. The F150's rear end begins to skid into my lane. He has hit black ice. The F150 continues to skid until it's at 180 degrees in the lane, and the rear end is well into my lane.

I slowly steer to the right, let up on the accelerator, and don't brake. F150 continues to turn rear end and is now 240 degrees facing me as I see the young man driver face me. We are now side by side with the truck facing oncoming traffic. The young man's eyes are the size of shiny marbles, and his hands are braced on the steering wheel. That image is frozen in my brain forever as the only one I will remember about our trip. It's a five-star rating personal experience and excitement on rush factor. I see Rosella brace her hand on the dash and hear her say oh my God. I have my eyes fixed on a truck's rear corner that is coming towards me and think here we go for impact. The F150 turned to almost 360 degrees and miraculously missed my front left by inches. As I turned to look to my left, I saw the F150 disappear. Looking forward, I was in the clear. Traffic all around me never missed a beat. I could not slow down but just hang on in a cold sweat. Rosella said nothing as we both moved along in shock.

At 100 km/h, we covered about 200 feet in about 2 seconds. To put this instant in perspective it's by far the most memorable of our trip. What a DAY so far and we are not even on the plane.

The slower traffic got us behind, and when we arrived at the airport, we were met by a Delta mobility assistant who had a cool access chair. That part was perfect, with a five-star rating for ease of access and attitude. However, the valet parking run by Westin was full, and I had to drive to park the car. As I made my way to the parking deck, I saw an attendant turning people away at the Valet parking entrance. I pleaded my case to, and attendant let me in. My luck was back with me. I got the last valet parking with the attendant not happy that I was let in. It took 30 minutes to get me a spot because they had to squeeze me in.

The check in took a while because Rosella had to be searched through the wheelchair entrance. We took the tram ride elevators and finally got to gate 20. We were supposed to be first in but ended up being last in. Vegas, here we come.

Vegas Airport is very disconnected, and it took forever to get to Hertz. The access chair ride, tram ride from Terminal 1 to 3, and bus ride to Hertz were a one-hour experience. Rosella never complained once. We arrived at Bellagio hungry and tired at 6:00 local time or 9:00 our time.

I knew that they had access to chair service but did not read the fine print. They only provide service from one location to another with their attendants. Access chairs are normally available, but they were all out. Apparently, things are getting busy for the Super Bowl on February 11th. As I waited at the bell desk, Rosella was in the rented car. The Bell person called for a wheelchair to one of her contacts. She told me that it would be $100 for delivery and $75/day.

I said let's get Rosella to the room with your service and then regroup. After another long wait to check in, Rosella got in the wheelchair at the Valet holding area. The young lady gave us a $50 restaurant pass for our wait. We are in room 27122 at 8:30 local time. Off I go to a snack bar to pick up 3 slices of pizza to be enjoyed with a $13 can of Sprite.

We might as well stay on the Bellagio theme. The next morning, as we sat at McDonalds next to our favorite Circus-Circus Hotel, I called a local wheelchair company. A man named Zach answered and said that he would deliver a unit to Bellagio by 9:00 a.m. for two days of use for a total of $75. We met him there and got the wheelchair into the SUV and off we went. Zach said that they deliver units there all the time. Then I thought about the bell person telling me that they were out and their contact would charge almost 3 times the price for the wheelchair!

That night, after a long day at Zion, we discovered that the bed was not made and the towels in the bathroom were not touched. I called for room service, and they came by and brought a shower chair for Rosella. After the bad pizza the day before, we ate snacks we picked up at a grocery store on our way back from Zion. We took in the fountain light show that is supposed to be the highlight. We were both disappointed at how short it was!

Before heading for the Grand Canyon, we decided to have our breakfast at the Bellagio Cafe. The outrageous price for two bagels and coffee, coupled with the stuck-up and condescending waiter's attitude, deserved a One Star rating. We paid our $35 and got the hell out.

After the Grand Canyon, we decided to use up our $50 at Spago Restaurant. We ordered a prosciutto and cheese platter. Again, the waiters were unhelpful and condescending. They helped little to sit Rosella down as if we were an inconvenience. The only saving grace was the bread tray! I really pissed the waiter off when I used the $50 gift certificate. Rosella wanted to give, not a tip. I left a $10 tip and got out of there too.

The last hurrah at the Bellagio was $20 at the slots. We found the cherries and 7's machine and lost $20 in $6 minutes! The genius of Vegas is simple. The slots only take cash. From the minute your cash goes in the slot, it's gone. I noticed that the cashier station was almost always empty, yet the slots were busy even at 6 a.m. The concept of taking cash from losers is brilliant. For this part, the Bellagio gets Five Stars.

Zion National Park:

The park is 2 ½ hours north of Vegas on I-15 in south Utah. It's a lush river valley carved into limestone that has the most beautiful colors we have ever seen. The summer is a crazy zoo of tourists, and you can only take tour trams. We were able to drive the whole route and have all the time we needed to enjoy the magnificent sights. Zion is a must see, and we would rate it as one of the best places we have seen in our travels. The park is Five Stars on natural beauty overload. We met a couple of our age from north Utah. The husband is a photographer and took our picture at the Court of Patriarchs.

Grand Canyon Skywalk –

The drive to the skywalk is 2 ½ hours south of Vegas in Arizona. The route has magnificent canyons with layers and layers of colors. The clear 65 deg F sunny day made it perfect. The Hoover Dam valley is on the way. We still have memories from our 1984 visit that allowed seeing the internal turbines. Ewe slowed down to see it but did not stop.

The Skywalk is owned by the Hualapai Indian tribe, and the drive goes through the reservation. Over one million visitors per year several go to it. On the way we saw Trump flags and got an appreciation of life on a poor and arid life. The experience is a must see for breathtaking views. The Joshua Tree Forest is one of a kind. The actual skywalk is very crowded, with many bust tours from all over the world. Overall, it's also a Five Star must see destination. Rosella got the royal treatment from bus driver Alejandro. He helped with easy access wheelchair movements into and out of the bus, including a lockdown mechanism for the drive.

March 8, 2025, email

Dear Chief Davis.

I would like to share with you my appreciation for 3 Memphis police officers who responded to a complaint at The Hilton Garden Inn Memphis Southaven on March 1, 2025, at about 10 pm. They came to our room to inform us that management had requested us to leave. They escorted us through a very angry crowd in the hotel that made us afraid for our lives. They were calm and professional, given the circumstances.

I have discussed the incident with Hilton management who agreed that the call to the police was initiated by guests. They claimed and believed that I was making their children uncomfortable. Two of the parents confronted me after returning from a short walk after driving all day from Louisville, KY. They requested I confirm that I was a guest there. I told them my room number and went to my room, thinking that it was strange for people to do that. Unbeknown to me, the hotel was full of parents there for a girl's baseball tournament. Hilton did their investigation and found no evidence of unusual activity. They have apologized and offered a refund.

We did see Graceland, but the experience was very traumatic in the hotel lobby. We truly believe your officers saved our lives that night and wish to share this good part of our trip with you. Please share this note with the officers.

I am 71, and my wife Rosella is 67. We came from Ontario, Canada, to see Graceland for a once in a lifetime experience.

Thank you

Angelo and Rosella

Reply by E-mail: Dear Angelo Ligori,

Thank you for taking the time to share your experience with us regarding the incident at the Hilton Garden Inn; we are grateful for your kind words about the three officers who responded to the situation. We strive to ensure the safety and well-being of our community and visitors, and your acknowledgment of their efforts reinforces our commitment to that mission. Thank you once again, and we hope to welcome you back to Memphis in the future.

Regards.

Memphis Chief of Police

At Graceland 2024

The Graceland trip officially put us in the "old" category. We did it for the experience and not because we are super Elvis fans. The Hilton experience will be with us for years.

Lost Money

Our move from Cornwall to Toronto was probably one of the most interesting experiences. We left Cornwall to go to Toronto. We talked to the bank manager in Cornwall. He assured us that everything was set up so that the money from our sale to the purchase in Toronto would be transferred to our TD account. We arrived in Toronto, and we arrived about 2 o'clock. The closing time was 4 p.m. We went to the TD bank and asked for a certified check to take it to our lawyer so that we could make the payment. When I went in there, I was informed by the teller that there was no money in our account. Somehow, the transfer that was supposed to have taken place didn't take place. We waited and searched and panicked for quite a while. The bank manager came out and said we had found it. We got our certified check, and eventually, we were able to pay the lawyer. Months later, at a family picnic, I ran into a cousin of mine who has the same name, Angelo Ligori. Somehow, we started talking about banks, and during the discussion; he mentioned that there was a strange transaction that happened. And the way it went, it appeared and disappeared. The amount was very large. He could never figure out what happened. And I told him what had happened. Somehow, they got the wrong Angelo. For a short moment, my Brantford cousin Angelo had the money, and we didn't. It did get found, and all was good. To this day, I still laugh over that because when it happened, my heart just sunk to my feet. What has happened here? But it all ended up well and we have a good laugh about it even today. Our Ligori family reunions are a tradition carried on for many years. Second cousin Fred Ligori has organized them for years. This picture below was taken in the mid 90's. Relations from as far as Montana were together. It's the story of Canada that brings immigrants together to share customs and make us so culturally rich.

Ligori Reunion 1996

My Scam

February 28, 2022, at around 11 a.m., I was called by TD Visa security. He said that Visa had two suspicious charges. One was an eBay watch that would be refunded. The other was a Master Card Joker cash card that needed to be traced by another security department. I was connected to a second person. He went on to explain that to trace these transactions, they needed my help because making more transactions through a secured TD account is the best way. I was told that TD Visa and Debit cards were canceled. I was given a new TD debit card number that I would need to pick up the next day at the bank. The current one could be used for transactions for the investigation. He told me that the breach happened at my bank, and they had my personal information.

He said that the investigation was well under way with the police file that he gave me. He also said that Olivia White had made the cash card purchase at No Frills. He asked that I help the investigation by purchasing a $1000 MC Joker Cash Card at No Frills. I drove to No Frills with the security person remaining on the phone. I bought the $500 card with my Debit Card. He told me that debit would work because the credit card was now blocked. At No Frills, I got $500 from a cashier named Mary. It was around 1 pm. on March 1st. I asked if there was an Olivia at the store. Mary said that she was there but away from registers. I did not confront him because the investigators said so. The store manager said that he could only sell $500 because of scams going on.

When I got back to the car, I told Kyle what happened, and he assured me that we were on the right track because he was aware of scams and now that we matched Olivia. He reassured me that I was really being helpful. He went on to tell me that my TD account was now secured from further tampering. They had set up a $7000 account that I was to use to trace any activity to catch the scammers. He also mentioned they had now confirmed an attempt to open a loan using my SIN, and there was an attempt to open a Bitcoin account. Kyle gave me case number 077186. He explained that a meeting with Ken Rodriguez at TD St. Clair branch is on Tuesday at 3 pm. At that meeting, I would receive $349 for my help, and all the funds used for purchases would be restored under file 0093421924. At that point, I was overcome either fear about the loan, the Bitcoin account, and the Olivia event, and I became even more determined to help with the investigation. I felt an obligation to help. I was also told that because of the SIN breach, my other credit cards could be breached as well.

After the No Frills purchase, I made a $2000 cash withdrawal from the TD St Clair branch. The teller, name Aimee, gave me the $2000. Also, TD assistant helped her to locate another $5000 at the King Street branch. The cash was used to buy cash cards and Shoppers St. Clair. I also agreed to buy more cash cards for $2000 with my MasterCard. The MasterCard case was given to me. I was told that once a SIN number was breached, other credit cards could be accessed.

I also did a $5000 withdrawal at the King Street branch. I saw teller Carrie Bechard. Kyle explained that these funds would be used for tracking down the attempted Bitcoin breach. I was sent a Bitcoin wallet QR code that allows me to deposit the funds at the Convenience Video outlet on St. Clair Street. Kyle reassured me that these withdrawals were coming from a secured account that was set aside and eventually refunded as part of the investigation. One last attempt that made me realize that something was not right was Kyle convincing me to buy more MCJOKER cards at the Superstore. By this time, MasterCard had blocked my card. The $2000 MCJOKER cards were flagged as suspicious.

By the time I realized all that had taken place, I had a terrible feeling that something was terribly wrong. I told Kyle that it had to end for the day. He told me to say nothing so that we would not compromise the investigation. We ended with Kyle telling me that he would call tomorrow to continue the investigation.

When I realized that there was clearly something wrong, I called CK Police and reported the events. I was told that it was all a scam and that the money was impossible to recover.

CHAPTER 9

Giving Back

The 2020 first planting of the river garden had a bumper crop of spaghetti and butternut squash. The highlight of the river garden was the 150-butternut squash crop. I filled 3 buckets and took them to the road with a mason jar. Total sales in 2020 were $78. The highlight of the sales was the $5 I got from one of my next-door neighbors. He came to hand deliver it after 5 years of not talking to me. We are friends again. The feud was about my sponsoring of the Grand River Bike trail. The best thing that happened to me all summer! Then came the idea of a garden club. Here are the experiences.

Gardens Mission: To experience the power of nature that can turn a seed into nutrition for our body and mind. We believe that as humans it's our duty to share with others so that we enable ourselves to be our best.

About us:

Mr. Angelo grew up in Italy, watching Nonno Gaetano grow fresh vegetables and bringing them to market. Years later Angelo has come full circle and grown some impressive vegetables. Angelo is a person who loves plants and cannot see them suffer. If you are that person, Angelo will mentor you with simple and hands methods you cannot get from YouTube. The experience will be especially valuable for young minds who are spending too much time in sedentary living. Learning by doing is a proven way that stays with everyone forever. It's especially powerful when done in the outdoors and not in a classroom.

Benefits of Gardening:

Angelo's Gardens is in a very fertile flood plain of the Thames River. You will find the riverbank location with access to the water very relaxing and a special experience. It is a way to relax and reduce stress from your busy life. From the May planting to the September harvest, the experience will be enjoyable and rewarding. There will be times when you will be truly overwhelmed with the bounty that nature will deliver to you.

The garden club experience brought out the natural human need to be with others after our lengthy pandemic absence from people. We are a social bunch and need others plus the outdoors to be happy. All that we do is from our desire to share the experiences we have with everyone. Here are some of the awards that kept us together.

1.   First Zucchini – Judee and Brian Glover – and the biggest zucchini. While all other plants were waiting for pollinators their zucchini exploded into first place.

2.   Best Looking Melons – Elise Hoekstra and Krissy Smith – no more can be said about this. Their melons go off to a pale start

after being moved from a science experiment at home but then become the talk of the gardens. The taste was outrageous.

3.   My Carrot is Bigger than Yours – Steve and Hazel Moore – for the straightest carrot and not at all mutant carrots that Angelo grew. The ward will be presented to Steve in the Greenfield maintenance shop, where many vegetable comparisons take place.

4.   Queen of the Ground Cherries – Emily Slavik – her gift comes from her family's dedication to the craft of ground cherry growing. Emily is destined to be an advisor to Ridgetown College, soon to be promoted to Dean. Emily also gets the weed shaming special mentions. Her plot got a bit weedy, so as part of my role I sent her a picture of her plot full of weeds. She was there the next day with Mya and Finn weeding away.

5.   Tomatillo Queen – Pat Riopel – introduced the new veggie that everyone fell in love with. Many new fans of tomatillos are now proud owners of salsas that will take us through winter. Pat is destined to achieve important things with her passion for new plant varieties started at home just after Christmas.

6.   Sucker Queens – Sherry Lenover and Susan Shaw –were the best at the hack and slash of the indeterminate tomato plants. Sherry mastered the art of pole driving without being hit by my sledgehammer. Susan has an uncanny ability to tell the difference between a leaf and a sucker.

7.   Youngest and Most Inquisitive – Luca Taylor and Jonnie McDiarmid-Sillers – it was wonderful to see the grandchildren in the garden. Luca and Jonnie brought a smile to all of us as they discovered with the biggest smiles ever.

8.   Best Kayak Rollover – Alex Thiel – who has never returned to the garden since after a quick splash in the river trying out an Olympic rollover.

9.   International Garden Award – Khagendra Ghimire – for introducing new vegetables that we have never grown before and cooking up an excellent stir fry. The highlight of the gardens is the Ghimire family. Their journey from their native county of Bhutan to our gardens is the purest example of the Canadian immigrant success story. A special thanks for the excellent vegetarian meal he cooked for us in the garage.

10.   Rookie of the Year Award. This year Rookie of the Year is presented to a most valuable and dedicated member! She demonstrated a cheerful outlook and a great interest and enthusiasm for all our varied activities. Got drenched during our tomato sauce ladies' day out. Our Rookie of The Year is none other than Pam!!!

11.   Although others dream of accepting the I'm On a Cruise Award, only one of our members truly deserves this designation! Craig is on a cruise right now. When he comes back, there are Cana lily bulbs to harvest. Three cruises and counting during the gardening season for the one and only Craig!!!

12.   King of Sweet Potatoes Award. This individual grew slips from scratch imported directly from The Caribbean! He came by the knee replacement physiotherapy to discuss the slip growing techniques and told me that you must cut the potatoes and put them in a jar of water. This year's King of Sweet Potatoes is our very own Amos!!

13.   The next award is another new addition to the FIFA World Cup year. It is the Lionel Messi Award, named after the best

professional soccer player who is the captain of the Argentinean national team! To qualify for this award, you must demonstrate similar greatness in your field and be of Argentinean descent. After careful consideration The Leo Messi Award goes to none other than Romina!!

14. The next award this evening is The Miss Congeniality Award! This award goes to the sweetest, most likable, and most amiable; nobody would ever say a bad word about.... none other than our sweet Linda!!! Linda was the first one to bring auction prizes.

15. The next award is The Queen of Cherry Tomatoes Award! No one else spent more time planting, tying, and spending a fortune of her own money on pipe cleaners to produce prize winning cherry tomatoes. She even threw out her back and has used up all our medical insurance! We are proud to present Susan as Queen of Cherry Tomatoes!

16. The next award is once again a brand-new category being, Ambassador of the Year. This individual brought in more members, encouraged visitors to the garden, and even made connections with interested individuals in England! The King of England may be showing up next!! For sure, we will have members from Ilderton next year, so I am told. The Ambassador of The Year Award goes to none other than Deanna!

17. Our next award is The Most Dedicated to Being a Couple Award! This duo shows up together, weeds together pull onions together, harvests together, leaves together.... they are basically joined at the hip! The Most Dedicated to Being a Couple Award goes to Deb and Cal McCabe!!

18. Our next award is the Wise Beyond My Years Award. This year's recipient is an individual who is mature, hardworking, intelligent, and even runs her own business. She may, in fact, be a 44-year-old disguised as a Grade 8 student!! Kudos to our Wise Beyond My Years Award...Mya!!!

19. The next award is The Queen Bee Award. This individual made Angelo watch The Bee Movie and is our resident bee expert. Did you know that bees have been around for 140 million years??? Females collect honey; males sit around until they eventually get eaten! Moral of the story...Don't Be a Male Bee!!! The Queen Bee Award goes to someone who is always busy as a bee.... Amanda!!!

20. Our next award is The Most Supportive Parents Award! This couple has spent countless hours supporting Country Markets Gardens putting in countless hours! If it wasn't for these two, The Country Markets stand would be floating down The Thames River!! Just ask Liz!!! She had a lot of fun one stormy, windy night!! Gary spent hours designing, building, and rebuilding the stand. We are proud to present The Most Supportive Parents Award to Liz and Gary!!!

21. The next award is fondly referred to as The Pizza Queen and King Award! This couple are experts at making delicious and authentic Italian pizza. They were so in demand this summer that they made pizza at a wedding for people they don't even know!! Just happened to be Angelo's next-door neighbor!!! How did that happen?? Pizza was supposed to happen between 9:15 and 11:00 p.m., but these two were still making the dough at 2:00 a.m.!!! Who does that??!!! Congrats to Emily and Steve....our Pizza Queen and King!!

22. Our next recipient is the winner of The Most Patient Wife Award!! This individual demonstrates patience and understanding of the hours that her husband puts into Country Markets Gardens. She even accompanies him on all emergency garden situations, which have been many this past growing season. Although Angelo and Rosella frequently spy headlights at all hours at the end of their driveway, they are not at all concerned! It's always Alex and his most patient wife......wonderful Paige!!!

23. Speaking of Alex....he is the proud recipient of our next award.... the irreplaceable Hori Hori Knife Award!! For those unfamiliar, this knife is a unique Japanese tool used only by expert gardeners. Let this award be the symbol that represents a successful 2024 Season. In 2024, Alex is now ready to take the leadership of Angelo's Gardens. We are more than proud to present the Hori-Hori knife to none other than our more than hard working Alex!!!

24. One member who had the best poses during the season when any picture was taken gets the Picture-Perfect Award. Judee was always well dressed in any picture. Most members are seen working, bending, and digging. Judee is posing and giving us the peace sign.

The article below captures our exciting venture so nicely. Author of the article: **Ellwood Shreve** Publishing date: Aug 04, 2021; **Angelo's Gardens brings young and old together to grow their own food.**

Growing up on a farm in Italy with his grandfather, who always had a large garden, and having a green thumb is in Angelo Ligori's genes. Having grown up on a farm in Italy with his grandfather, who always had a large garden, a green thumb is in Angelo Ligori's genes.

So as the COVID-19 pandemic dragged on, it didn't take much convincing for Ligori to take the lead in creating the Angelo's Gardens co-operative in the backyard of his expansive property. "The idea is a rent-a-plot," said Ligori, adding there are some options on what people can do.

"You can either plant your own (vegetables) or look after it for a fee, or I have some platinum members. I look after most of the plots, and they simply come and get their veggies once a week," he said.

Pat Riopel, her husband Enrico Magnani, and their children, Bruno, 2, and Valentina, four months, are members of the cooperative. Riopel, who met Ligori at a Chatham YMCA fitness class, said she suggested he start the co-operative after seeing his own large garden.

"I think when COVID hit, he needed a project," she said. "As ambitious as he is, he got himself into a big project, and everybody's happy about it – it's amazing," Riopel said; her family is a platinum member, but she hopes to get more involved in the planting and harvesting when their children get a little older. She is impressed with the results. "I didn't think the vegetables could get that big." Ligori said about three-quarters of an acre was planted for this growing season but noted there is room for more members. He said the "coolest part" for him is sharing his knowledge of gardening.

Alex Wingrove, who owns and operates Country Market Garden across the Thames River on Riverview Line, has enjoyed learning from Ligori as they share duties in running the cooperative. "I've learned what a small idea can turn into if it's someone like Angelo, who's passionate about it and works hard at it," he said. Wingrove, who has seen his own business grow in five years from a "hobby garden" into a full-fledged business that supports a family, recalled when he saw Ligori's post on Facebook about the cooperative.

"I thought it was just going to be a simple, rent some land and harvest crops, but it turned into something much better." He said there's been a lot of knowledge shared among the small community of gardeners in the co-op.

"I'm always happy to share information and teach people how to grow things," he added. Tricia Weese and her son Brennan, 8, are among the families that have joined Angelo's Gardens. "We thought it would give us something to do for the summer, and it would be a good learning experience for everybody," Weese said. She grew up on a farm where there was always a vegetable garden, but she said there's just not enough room where they live in the city.

Brennan proudly chimed off the vegetables they were growing, which included tomatoes, jalapeno peppers, green peppers, beans, cauliflower, and peas. However, Brennan also noted the reality of gardening in Southwestern Ontario. "I am getting mosquito bites," he said. But he's also making a few bucks, having sold $51 worth of vegetables via YouTube.

Angelo's Gardens has given Mary DeKoter a chance to get back into growing her own food. Having grown up with a father who was an avid gardener, growing potatoes, beans, and tomatoes, she said she decided to "just get right in there" when she heard about the cooperative on Facebook. She shares some of her bounty with the food bank. DeKoter hopes more young families will get involved in Angelo's Gardens. "It's a lost art, but I think it's coming back because the price of food is going to go up with COVID," she said.

The garden plots were a hobby just covering costs. It did bring about the new venture of Alex moving his Country Market Garden small business to our lot. It's the beginning of a new chapter.

The Trail Speech: January 28, 2020

Mayor Darrin Canniff, Council, Ladies and Gentlemen....

I am happy to be here to recall that beautiful day last August when we dedicated the bench for Phase 1 of the River Trail. I continue to believe that Greenfield's support aligns with many of our values. Our President, Howard Field, shares this same vision. Howard has used the trail many times when he visits.

The trail will be 21 km and a perfect course for a healthy community. I am sure that it will add a huge positive for tourists. I am equally confident that walking, running, and cycling will be much easier to access for many residents, including our employees.

The trees along the riverbanks have some of the oldest cottonwood stands in SW Ontario. Some sections with water and trees show nature at its best. The local cycling clubs would be delighted to use the trail because it will make it much safer for them. The route is one of the most popular ones for CK cyclists.

I would like to express my personalized message to the council. Please consider the generations in the future that will be healthier, live longer and happier in our community. I am certain that they will thank you for making the right decision.

This bench is dedicated to Angelo Ligori. It is in honor of his 17 years of service to Greenfield Global Incorporated and to recognize his unwavering commitment to completing the Thames River Trail in 2022. The trail was inspired by his wife Rosella's cycling accident in 2010. We thank you for your invaluable contributions to the company and your steadfast dedication to creating a healthy and safe community space for all.

The River Trail brought the best of our community spirit. The event in the article below shows how the life of one family was impacted. Its moments like this that I live for.

Memorial bench honours memory of Austin Scott; reminder of importance of pathways to community

Author of the article: **Ellwood Shreve**, Published Nov 09, 2020

A memorial bench has been installed along the Greenfield Global Trail on Bloomfield Road in Chatham to honour the memory of Austin Scott.

Austin died at age 18 after being struck by a vehicle while riding his bicycle on the evening of Nov. 25, 2015. Pictured in front are his sister Alissa Scott, 21, left, and Mother Jenn Scott during a ceremony on Sunday. Pictured from back left are Angelo Ligori, senior advisor with Greenfield Global, Neil Bishop, Greenfield Global vice-president of operations, Greg Devries and Hilco Tamminga, partners in Truly Green Farms greenhouses, and Jeff Bray, manager of parks and open spaces with the Municipality of Chatham-Kent. jpg, CD

Jenn Scott lost her 18-year-old son Austin after he was struck by a vehicle while riding his bicycle at night on a busy section of Bloomfield Road nearly five years ago. Today, she hopes the same tragedy won't happen to others on the same stretch of roadway.

Scott, along with daughter Alissa, 21, and family and friends, were joined Sunday by officials from Greenfield Global and Truly Green Farms greenhouses, as well as Chatham-Kent recreation staff, for the dedication of a memorial bench in Austin's honour along a multi-purpose trail that runs adjacent to Bloomfield Road, between Riverview Line and Richmond Street.

"We know with this being done, his memory can live on," Scott said. "We can hopefully save other lives down here. The memorial bench stemmed from a chance meeting between Jenn and Alissa Scott and Angelo Ligori, a senior adviser at Greenfield Global, shortly after Austin died on Nov. 25, 2015.

"It was a cold November night, and I saw them there (putting up a cross at the crash site) and I stopped, and I went over and said, 'I'm so sorry to hear about your son,'" Ligori recalled. He said Jenn Scott gave him a hug before he got back in his car to continue his journey home from the ethanol plant, located across from where the tragedy occurred.

About a year ago, Ligori saw Jenn again, "and she said, 'I know you from somewhere.' "He said they talked about the night they first met and how Scott was pleased to see the multi-use trail and lighting that has been put up on Bloomfield Road.

"Austin would be alive today if that trail had been there," Ligori remembered Scott saying. "She brought me to tears." Ligori told Scott that Greenfield Global is the major sponsor of the Round the River Recreational Trail and believed the municipality owed the company a bench.

Since the fatal collision, Bloomfield has also undergone a major reconstruction, including the installation of plenty of street lighting. Ligori said Greenfield Global had the municipality's engineering team over to the plant while the company's safety co-ordinator and Truly Green folks gave advice as well.

"A lot of what's taken in place on Bloomfield goes back to Austin, for sure," he said. Scott said her family was "grateful" for the community's support, adding her son "would be happy." They came together and they did this," she said. Genevieve Champagne, Chatham-Kent's active transportation and special events co-ordinator, said this type of memorial bench is a way "to remember why these pathways are important to the community." "It was really a big deal for us to get that multi-use pathway in for cyclists, so they have a safer transportation method," she said about the trail that was installed last year.

The goal is to allow people to get anywhere in Chatham by bicycle on safe, active transportation routes, she added. "We're excited. It's all through our master plans," Champagne said.

15 Minutes of Fame

My Run CK Friends

For the past five years, area run organizers have been working together to try to ensure every event wins when it reaches the finish line. This has been achieved through the creation of the RunCK series, which includes a website through the Chatham-Kent web portal at www.chatham-kent.ca.

Local runner Angelo Ligori saw that several organizations were holding runs, so he said, "I got them all together and said, 'Maybe we should do something as a group.'" He noted Chatham-Kent helped to develop a web page as a one-stop location to promote and provide information on the several runs that take place across the municipality.

Tom Slager, director of resources for the United Way of Chatham-Kent, said being part of RunCK has created a lot of "schedule stability, which is great." He said all the runs are scheduled around the same time, including the United Way's Harvest Run on Sept. 24, so "it just makes it really easy for everybody to plan, and you know you're not stepping on toes." Noting it takes months to plan these events, which could be negatively impacted if two are happening at the same time, Slager said, "it just works out really good that we're all on the same page."

Amy Wadsworth, general manager of the Chatham-Kent YMCA, said the agency's Family Fun Run/Walk kicks off the run series on April 30."It's really important to be part of the RunCK series because it shows community effort; all of us working together with one common goal – to get as many people in our community active," she said." That's really what the RunCK series is working towards," she added. Wadsworth said proceeds from the YMCA's race go to its Strong Kids charity "so that we can help as many in our community as we can who need that hand up."

This is the fifth year for the Run for Mental Health event, being held May 13, to support programs offered through the Mental Health Network of Chatham-Kent. Program supervisor Jenny Jackson said a major benefit of being part of the run series is the collaboration between the race organizers. "We can learn other best practices . . . and what works and doesn't work, so that's a huge bonus," she said. Jackson has seen plenty of repeat participants in several of the races.

"I've done pretty much every run in the RunCK series, and I've noticed that you have those that run all of the races, and you have people who just come out for certain ones, or what can fit into their schedule," she said.

Mark Childs, with the Defiance Running Club of Wallaceburg, helps organize the WAMBO Run, being held on Aug. 12, and the Jingle Bell Run on Dec. 9. When asked if he's noticed the popularity of running increase, Childs said it's not just more people who are getting into running. "There's more walkers out there," he said. "Activity, in general, has increased tenfold from five years ago. "Our club has seen a big surge," he added, noting it peaked at 192 members. Childs said there is a social aspect to the Defiance Running Club with people making good friends.

While there are competitive runners, including some who train for marathons, he said the goal is to include everyone. "If you can't run, don't worry about it, come out and walk."

Discovered Human Remains

January 11, 2024, 3:26 p.m.

This official notification of found human remains is located at 6914 Grand River Line, Chatham.

Remains were discovered by a construction company using a backhoe to dig to install a geothermal heating/cooling system. They are in the backyard of this property, quite close to the Thames River, on land that used to be agricultural. The remains are quite close to the surface and exhibit evidence of old as well as new breaks. The old breaks suggest a disturbance in the past. There are multiple individuals represented, and nothing could be seen in articulation. Bones were dumped from the bucket on the edge of the excavation and bones remain within the trench and soil. Some teeth were viewed, and they exhibit attrition.

These remains are those of Indigenous individuals buried in an ossuary. Police will attempt to cover the exposed remains if possible. The construction company has halted all digging and left the scene. They would like to retrieve the heavy equipment that they are renting, and I have told the police that it is okay for them to do so, provided that all soil is left behind. The homeowners are aware that they will be responsible for protecting the remains until they receive further direction, and the homeowner, Mr. Angelo Ligori, is copied here.

The regional and chief coroners are copied here, and they can give the required info to Crystal. I was sent 76 photos of the site, so I am not attaching them here. Please let me know if there is anything else I can do. Please consider this my report on the matter.

Forensic Anthropologist

Forensic Services and Coroner's Complex

Chatham Daily News: Published Jul 06, 2024, **by** Ellwood Shreve

Angelo Ligori said he and his wife, Rosella, decided to try a geothermal project after successfully installing a solar panel project on the roof that now sends power back to the grid. He said while excavating the second line for the geothermal project, "is where we hit the human remains." The ossuary, a type of First Nation burial site, was "just nicked" when the area was being dug using heavy machinery, Ligori said. "That's what was visible when we brought the bucket up," he added.

He said the project was stopped immediately, and the contractor was very diligent in providing the necessary legislation and explaining what needed to happen. Ligori said the process began in January, which initially involved the police, leading to an investigation under the Funeral, Burial and Cremations Services Act.

The couple have engaged a "very reputable company," Archaeology Research Associates, to assist them. Ligori also reached out to several First Nations in the area to become involved. Caldwell First Nation Chief Mary Duckworth is impressed with how Ligori has handled the situation. "I think it was a very lovely experience to meet Angelo because he was so open, so honest," she said. "What I gleaned from it more than anything, he wanted to do the right thing, and he wanted to build relationships."

An investigation has been ongoing at the property of Angelo and Rosella Ligori after the remains of four Indigenous adults, and two children were discovered while a geothermal project was underway at their property along the Thames River west of Chatham. Duckworth said what is known about the discovery is there were four adults and two children buried on the property. "It looks like this could be part of an ossuary that's why more investigation needs to happen," she said.

She added the investigation is still in the preliminary stage. Ligori said experts he's spoken to are not exactly sure how old the remains are at this point, but they are believed to be pre-War of 1812. Duckworth said this is the third time in the last three years she has been involved with the discovery of First Nation remains. Once was in the Leamington area, and the other was at Point Pelee National Park, she added.

The Chief said both discoveries "turned out great because, again, it was a joint effort to notify the Nations and be able to speak to the archeologist and be able to come out and honor (those found buried) by doing a ceremony."

Ligori never considered for a moment to just bury the remains to avoid having to deal with everything that stems from this type of discovery. This is despite the fact the couple could face a significant cost as the investigation continues. The couple has made an application to the province for "undue financial hardship" to cover the costs.

If remains are just covered back up, Duckworth said, "I think you must put that in the context of the settler population. "If it was your own relatives or people that had lived here, don't they all deserve the same respect?" she added.

The remains have been removed from the site, but it still needs to be determined what will happen with them. "We'll wait to hear more, and then we will make decisions based on that," Duckworth said. Ligori said one option is to return the remains and erect something to mark the burial site on the property. He added the story continues, noting officials will be returning to investigate further because artifacts, including pottery and an arrowhead have been found during the investigation.

Little red flags dot the property around the burial site where more investigation will take place. "There is a sign here that someone was here a long time ago," Ligori said.

The aboriginal excavations took place from June to October 2024.

First Nations observers oversee the Archeology Technicians as they carefully excavate and screen the area, looking for either human remains or artifacts.

Sister Mary

The burial site experience brought something back to mind that all has to do with connecting with people. Part of the investigation involves meeting with the First Nations elders that will help identify the grave site and what needs to be done next. Very early in the process, I ended up meeting with Mary Duckworth, Chief of the Caldwell Nation. We met on a rainy day. I brought her to the location, and while we were taking our golf cart ride to the location, we started talking. She mentioned that her name was Mary Frances, and she was raised a Catholic, just like I was. Her mom wanted her to be a nun. So, it made me laugh because I mentioned that my mom also wanted me to be a priest. I was going to be called Padre Angelo. We laughed a little bit, and, from that point on, Mary helped me very much with all the work that needed to be done to conclude the archaeological First Nations excavation. I find that if you have some common background on how you want to approach a problem, you can do it very well. Mary went on to help me with how to possibly amend the act that involves finding human remains on your property. I will take that first meeting where the two of us have something in common and then what we did with it. If you find common bonds, two people can accomplish anything together. If there is no common bond or meeting of the minds, there will never be accomplishments.

The burial site discovery taught me so many lessons about what is going on in our world today, starting with the huge discrepancy between us, the white people that are here, and what happened a few thousand years ago in the lands of the First Nations. We have come here with our traditions and bulldozed over everything that was here for thousands of years. However, during my learning of the excavation, I found out that the traditions that are held by the First Nations are extraordinarily strong and very powerful and should remind us that we perhaps may have taken a wrong turn, as Western civilization.

The laws that right now are attempting to fix mistakes that were made hundreds of years ago. However, undoing legacy mistakes takes a long time. FBCSA that we had to follow to get the burial site remediated was very arduous and exceedingly difficult for us. A lot of the people that I talked to did not agree with me following all the requirements. Most would have put the bones back in the ground and not said a thing. I was not looked upon favorably by a few people who believe that we are here, and it doesn't matter what was here before us.

We are human, and we should show respect for all others. The traditions of the First Nations are strong, including one powerful one. During the burial site remediation, the First Nation's female elder who put the bones back packed them in by hand. She told me that their tradition is "women bring us to earth, and women put us back to earth." It's a powerful statement that is at the root of human existence on this earth and should be remembered by all of us. This tradition is not as artificial as most modern religions. It's the order of nature.

The burial site taught me that lesson in many ways. I also want to refer to the beginning of the story, where my mom taught me that you should respect everything that happens in your life. Always do the right things that are proper even when no one is looking. That is the definition of integrity.

The elders also taught me that the cottonwood tree that's on our property that's 150 years old is revered. Its roots were here a long, long time ago when our First Nations were here. So, I got reminded that perhaps at some point, my ashes belong right here because that's the way our ancestors were put back to earth. That's truly the way life goes on this earth. So, it's a philosophy of what I believe.

Through time, I've come to learn that there are so many other beliefs of humankind, and I have been open minded about them. Organized religion has pacified us into the illusion of everlasting life. Religious fanaticism is not always the way of life. My God is better than yours cannot be true. We are here to live one lifetime with integrity and honesty as our religion. I believe we are stardust.

CHAPTER 10

Admirable People and Times

Al Fox:

Excavations and the Aboriginal ossuary discovery in our backyard that will follow will be entertaining. I must take you back a few decades because, as one would have it, excavations always bring surprises. This experience takes me back to nightmares of a 1994 project that I did with BASF, building a primer plant in Windsor. My partner was Al Fox. He was with me through the whole terrible time. The $20 Million project was estimated to cost about $400,000 for the civil foundation alone. As we were excavating, we uncovered that there had been a fire, and back in the 50s, they had buried it all, and in there was contaminated soil, and there were some nastiest, including strontium and chromium. Those are very nasty substances that cannot be left. After dealing with the Ministry of the Environment and the lengthy reviews, we ended up spending six months and nearly a million dollars to remediate everything back so that we could build the plant. That experience put the project nearly 30% over budget and six months behind schedule. I found out that BASF does not like cost overruns and delays. I had to write a report explaining all of that. I remember the night I drafted the report; it was a Friday night, and I knew that by Monday, I would hear some news that was not very pleasant. It was a sunny day that I remember as I was driving out of the plant. I thought to myself, if I go south of the border, I will be able to find a place to live. It will be south of the border, and I will drive as far as I can. Hopefully, by Monday, I will be far away and not easy to get a hold of. I wanted so badly to do that; however, I went home, spent the weekend, and on Monday, I got my call basically telling me that they understood, and I found out later that the project was successful. However, during that period, it was not easy to know all these uncertainties. We eventually started up the plant with numerous deficiencies. Al Fox shook my hand and made a batch of primer paint before Christmas, as we promised. A feeling of accomplishment between two people is always about trust.

My BASF experience did bring more people that made me a better person. Tom McKay showed me a perfect balance of intelligence and humility. We spent years in our search to improve profitability and while making tough decisions on peoples' lives. Tom used has charm and with intelligence that amazed me. We covered USA locations with cultures only he could navigate. My admiration for him remains forever. Working for a German company tested every ounce of brain power. Hope is not a strategy still brings a smile to both of us. The sentence was used at a meeting where we were presenting a strategic plan to the global director of our division. During the presentation, the USA VP said, "We hope that our pricing strategy holds". The global director calmly said, "Hope is not a Strategy". The room went quiet and ended quickly.

As we left the room one of the other USA team members said. Today the IQ of 3 of us did not add up to the one we talked to.

Dr. McLaughlin:

Engineering at UWO continued to be a struggle for me the first year when all we were doing was trying not to get weeded out. We started with 400 people, and we graduated there were 107 of us. Through that weeding process, Calculus and Electric circuits were mandatory. Electricity and I don't get along at all. I got 59% on my first-year midterm exam. I was so devastated by that mark. I went to see the legendary Dr. McLaughlin, who later got a building named after him at the University of Western Ontario. Dr. McLaughlin had what you would call a monumental presence in its own time and place. He was kind of king of the engineering school. Everybody respected him.

However, I got enough courage to go and ask him to see if he could give me an extra mark so that I would get a 60. After a lengthy discussion, going back and forth, he asked me what discipline I was going into, and I said chemical. He paused and said, "Mr. Ligori, I will give you a 60, but I never want to see you in the electrical wing ever again in our industry. Have a good day, sir". That was the end of that conversation. I still remember that meeting very, very much. It took a lot of courage for me to do that, but I got my 60. Every time I saw Dr. McLaughlin in the halls, he did say hello to me.

Alan Jeffs

Engineering is a discipline that, through school, teaches you to be part of a team. In my second year, I was fortunate enough to form a team with three other classmates in chemical engineering at Western who graduated together. Jim Covert, Dave Hinkley. Alan

Jeffs, and I were friends and competitive. Each one of us had a special gift to get things done as a team. Jim was organized and well prepared, with a curiosity that was immense. Jim went on to be an excellent computer controls expert. Dave was the hard-working local person who lived at home and yet got so much done and helped our team succeed. He has traveled all over the world on energy projects. Alan Jeffs was the brain of the group, and he was the one whenever we had all the difficult moments that engineering gives us; we would go to a class and use the Whiteboard, and he would single-handedly produce answers to problems that in the fourth year, we were using stuff that we took in the first year. Alan is a brilliant person whom we admired immensely; by the way, his sidekick used to go to Western Raceway in between classes and went a few races, and he ended up paying for his university with his skill set just gives you an idea of the team that I ended up with. To this day, I still stay in touch with Jim, Dave, and Alan as the three people who got through the profession and contributed immensely to our society.

John Fisher

When I joined Shell for the very first time in Sarnia I recall walking by John Fisher's office. John is the plant manager; I could see that one morning, he was reading the Globe and Mail and had his feet up on his desk and he was smoking a pipe. I looked in, and I could see Lucille Dark, his personal secretary. I had thought that someday, I wanted to be just like that. It was 1978. I decided back then that I wanted to be a plant manager just like John Fisher, have my own secretary, have an office with a bathroom, and have an office with a bar.

Fast forward, and 30 years later I finally became plant manager of the ethanol plant in Chatham. We were told that we were supposed to be retiring at 55. Freedom 55 was the 80s message we got. It was said to us, and I was going to have all the wonderful things of life. 32-hour work weeks and a plush life as rewards for our hard work. As plant manager, I had no secretary. I had a tiny office with no bar. If I wanted to have my coffee, I had to get it myself down the hall and use the coffee machine that everybody else used. Between 1978 and 2008 and 30 years later, that is what happened to my dream of becoming a plant manager, reading the Globe and Mail, and having my own personal secretary. Life does bring surprises, for sure. Upon reflection and observing the waves of Gen X, Millennial, and Gen Z, there is a clear shift to the enjoyment of life mindset. The parts I treasure are moments when I'm called the OG. The first thing I thought was they were calling me Old Guy. I learned that it means Original Gangster. It's a term of respect for wisdom brought into the conversation of today.

When we moved back to Ontario, I tried to recover, but then the weight came on, and as you will hear, Dr. Spiro clocked me with a little bit of pudginess. I hit 196 pounds in the mid-90s, and that was the time that I decided, okay, I am going to run my world marathons. I did so much running that I continued to bang up my knee. After Boston, I had to slow down, and I went through so many chiropractors that the list is too long to list, but two really helped me. One was Paula Radovich in Windsor. She got me to Boston, and I'm not sure how many needles and procedures I got from her. In Chatham, I met Dr. Sarah Yitzma. Sarah has worked on every part of my body, hamstring, heel, knee surgery recovery, massage therapy, needles, laser, consultant, and advisor. The epic memory is the day she brought her two boys to the house for a visit. Younger Everet decided to take a drink from our outdoor decorative water fountain. He is mow all grown up and just fine! Now, I'm at the point where it's just maintenance to get me through the rest of the way. That was a journey. It all started with my knee injury back in 1978.

Of course, my tales cannot go without the Spin with Angelo decade that I'm still going through. This started in 2010 when I joined the YMCA. We had some classes at 6 a.m. On a chilly winter day, the instructor never showed up. Judee Glover, one of the people that were in the class, said, "Angelo, get up there and see if you can teach us." 13 years later, I've been going at it. We've now got a little cult going because I have got quite a few people who are still coming from the original clan. Now, it's become a social get-together where we tell tales, sweat a little, and talk about all kinds of life experiences.

We raised $10,000 by doing Angelothon charity events. The catalyst was Andrew Thiel, who got us sponsors, flyers, food, and awards. Pat Riopel brought out the entire Scribendi Team. The events were 15 minutes of Spin bike, 15 minutes in the pool, and a one-mile run followed by awards. T Shirts are still out there, and it's become a legendary event.

Tunes like Hash Pipe, Sandstorm, and Moves like Jagger are favourites. I was able to recruit most of the Spin class to join the Garden Club. Many chats are about growing vegetables. Prizes given are mostly vegetables or fruit. So, it's a very nice way to socialize and back off from my days in the running to now something a little bit more, less impact for my body. And my knee likes it a lot better.

My Spin Class Team 2015

Dad Giovanni

A little bit of information about Dad and what we went through with me growing up. Giovanni went to grade 3, and then World War 2 came along. His life changed forever. Pofi was in the where the Germans made their last stand. As the Allies came through Pofi, his town was nearly destroyed. He told me stories about the war that seemed unreal. One of his relatives was killed by a Moroccan soldier. I used to walk by a cross near our house in Pofi where that man was buried. He could feel the earth shake as the Allies bombed Montecassino. My dad was hardened by the war to a point where most would not understand. After the struggles in the 50s, commuting 100 km each way from Pofi to Rome as a carpenter, his job at Heinz was a luxury. Dad worked at Heinz his whole life. He sweated and worked so hard that he was our backbone and kept the family going. While in high school, the topic of "What u want to do when you grow up?" came up a lot. One Easter meal, we were all there, me, Mom, Dad, Toni, Stef, and Anna. The topic came on to what a career should be for Angelo. For some reason, that day, Dad was insistent that I become a hairdresser. He, at the time, along with

177

all the Italians in Leamington, was getting their haircuts going to Pasqualino. He did the hair for men, women, and everyone. Dad believed that it was cash money and that it would be the business that would be good for Angelo. I said, "Dad, I don't want to do that. I want to go into engineering and go to university". He got up, left, and went to the cantina. We never saw him for a while. My sisters all looked at me and said, there you go, Angelo, you upset Dad.

Time moved on. I graduated. I came back and told Dad that I was going to be working at Shell in Sarnia as a process Engineer. He looked at me at me and said, "All this time, you get a job at the gas station"? So, I said, Dad, no, that is not what I do. I am going to work at the refinery in Sarnia. And there, I'll have my job. He looked at me and said, ah, you are going to be one of those guys with the white shirts and ties. Of course, at Heinz, he had industrial engineers walking around, optimizing the plant. He related my job to putting people out of work. I will never forget that conversation, but he did leave me with this. He said, "Angelo, when you are big boss, you make sure that you do not do what I see. You must believe that the fish rots from the head". The translation is that a leader should always follow integrity and good values. To this day, I still remember that conversation that took place when I was about 16 years old. I have done my best to live my life with honesty, integrity, openness to change, and respect for others.

All my love of gardening must go back to not only my grandfather but also my dad, Giovanni. Dad is the one that I found bearing a fig tree when he was 86. The hole that he was digging was deeper than his height, and he was doing that to bury the fig tree so that it wouldn't freeze. And he had that fig tree for years. I remember watching this and thinking oh my goodness, what's he doing? I've inherited a fig tree that he gave me. I'm still enjoying it. He grew a

35 lb watermelon that, to this day, I've never seen one that big, and it was delicious. All the tools that we moved from his house on Melrose Avenue are now in my shed. The Leamington Heinz workforce was mostly Italian. The hardest working person that I've ever known, Dad worked long hours in the pickle department '70s, '80s, and '90s to retirement. Leamington is still embedded in memories as the Tomato Capital. I can say to you that Pride, hard work ethic, and love of his family are what made Giovanni an incredibly special person. I recall being introduced to the Bank Manager the day we went to open a joint bank account. I spent 10 minutes at the bank, being proudly introduced to all the tellers. All I needed to do was co-sign one document.

Giovanni is the Watermelon King

Toni

My sister Antonia, or as we call her Toni is the one I have that is the classic definition of a social person that loves Good Times, loves parties, loves children, loves friendship and life. I recall going to see her at the University of Windsor residence. As I made my way down the hall, as soon as I mentioned that I was Toni's brother, everyone joined me as I made my way to her room. It was almost noon, and she had just got up. Time passed, and I was then named "Toni's Brother". We spent many years at a Chinese restaurant named Shin-Shin. The owner knew Toni as a regular customer. My name was too hard to pronounce for the Cantonese restaurant owner, so every time I called to make a reservation, I was "Toni's Brother."

Toni is level-headed and straightforward. She is loved by so many people that I've run into in life. I recall one friend that I ran with for quite a few years. Toni's name came up, and I came to find out that he was taking a course at the University of Windsor that my sister was teaching. All that I could hear from Mario was how wonderful Toni was as a person and professor. Those memories are still with me after so many years.

Stefania

We came to Canada with my mom, dad, and my two sisters, Toni and Anna. And lo and behold, in Canada, in 1968, we welcomed a new member to the family. And how this happened was quite odd because we were a little bit older. I was 15, and very late during my mom's pregnancy, we found out that she was going to have another baby. I personally was very shocked because I had already moved on thinking that that was all of us. When Dad came home from the hospital, he mentioned that we had a baby girl. He was intent on naming her Joanna for Giovanni. However, at the time, I was in grade school, grade 8, and it was at the time that I had a crush on her. After a lengthy discussion, and me not really liking Joanna, we named her Stefania. To this day, I still remember that conversation. It was a hot June day, and we were discussing it back and forth. And to this day, Stefania and I still have a chuckle over that because she is named after one of my girlfriends. Stefania grew into her time, and I do recall that when she was three or four, and I had my high school buddies playing poker in the basement, which was the talk of all of us. We have quite a big age gap between us and her, to the point that I've still to this day been considered by her as a father figure because of our age gap. So, that is a story that will still bond us together for years to come.

Anna:

I'm four years older than Anna, so we chummed around a lot, and I carried her on my back a lot back in the Italian farms. And I still recall some of our childish experiences, one of which, to this day, I still can't believe that she is alive. What we were doing was I was on the very top landing of a 15-step marble concrete stairwell that went to the second story of where we lived. And I was sitting on the one side of the landing. She had a little tiny child's chair. She was on the other side of me on the landing. And I kept asking Anna to move back a little bit more, move back a little bit more, because she was blocking the sun, and I wanted to be in the sun. Well, the last part I remember is the two hind legs of the little chair were not on this landing anymore. As she went over, I could see that she had fallen, and all I remember was watching something like a rag doll completely going head over foot, head over foot, tumbling and landing at the very bottom of the landing of the stairs. And at that moment, I remember looking down. She was not moving, and I thought for sure we had lost Anna. However, as two-and-a-half-year-olds go, she was fine. She was bruised. Mom came to help. There was a lot of crying by both of us. To this day, Anna, I still believe that we may have done something that day, but now it's a moment of laughter compared to that time, which was a very terrifying experience.

The women of my life are Rosella, Toni, Stefania, Anna, and Mom. Caterina is special in a very different yet complimentary way. Their love and care for me have contributed to making life fun and enjoyable.

Uncle Luigi:

After my summer of 2003 Madrid airport lost luggage experience, I finally did land in a Rome airport. It's called Fiumicino. My uncle, Luigi, and Aunt Assunta were there to pick me up. It was after midnight. It was a Friday night. And as we got into the little, tiny Fiat, I was in the front seat. My aunt is in the back, and Luigi is driving. We are going towards downtown Rome. The streets were not that full, however. For a while, I had this feeling that something was weird, but then I realized that because I was tired, and each time there was a red light, he would go through it. We went through one red light after another after another. Finally, I said in Italian, Zio, why are you going through a red light? He said, "In Rome, red lights are just a warning. If there's no one coming, we just keep going". That was my first experience of Italian driving. The next day, he drove me to our little town called Pofi. Along the Autostrada we were doing, it was already a Saturday morning, it was very busy. We were doing 120 following vehicles in front of us that were so close. It had garbage in it. It's the big clamps that you could see all the garbage on the truck. I could read the labels on the wrappers of garbage that were in the truck. That's how close we were, and we were doing 120.

Luigi and Giovanni are 10 years apart and share a special bond, being the oldest and the youngest of the Ligori family.

Fast forward, we go to Pofi. I was there for a weekend, and it was in August 1996 the temperatures in our little town in mid-August were 37 to 40 Celsius during the day, and at night, it cooled to 30. Back then, I was running, so in the morning, I remember I had just one carry-on with shorts on. My aunt had washed my shorts. I went for my morning run, and I went very early, and it was already so warm that I did not run far because one the heat. Two, in our small town, there are no leashes on dogs. Dogs just run around, and they really love to chase runners. So, I went half a mile and saw a pack of dogs, some of which had patches missing from their bodies, and they had their teeth out growling away, and all I did was just turn around and go back home.

I sat up until noon. I sat up until about 9 o'clock when everybody was waking up, because, in Italy, everybody goes to bed at midnight and 1 o'clock and does not get up until 10. By that time, everybody got up, and they asked me what I had been doing, and I said I was just getting my son. So that was probably the most memorable experience of my Italian trip back in a sweltering summer. And the other part, that is, also hilarious, is my trip to the Vatican. The trip to the Vatican was about an hour, and it was my uncle as a tour guide. He parked in a no-parking spot where they were doing construction. A whole bunch of Italian men came out yelling and screaming at him. He got in the car. He told me to get in and drove off, and, he said in Italian; I'm not sure what's wrong with them, but this is basically the Italian and Roman way. No one respects the rule of law. However, it is all innocent, and everyone is just at the edge of, I call it, being courteous, but they have their ways of getting things done.

I have a personality that that wants to save the world. However, I do not listen to my body as it tries to do so. In 2017, after I retired from work, I was doing part-time consulting. Mrs. Mattei, my mother-in-law, was ill. She was hospitalized, and we realized that she could no longer live alone. We decided to sell the house and have her move in with us while I was already taking care of Rosella after all her neurosurgery experiences. And as well, my son Daniel was still living at home. So, for a while, between my mother-in-law, my wife, and my son, it got very complicated for me to get through my daily life to a point where most people around could tell that I had become very irritable and unable to make sound decisions. And after a long thought on my own, I decided to see a counselor. When I went to see the counselor, one of the tests we did was a Beck Depression survey, and for each question that you answer on a 0 to 3 scale, the more you are depressed and the more points you score. So, they ask questions: how often do you have sleepless nights? How often do you worry about others, etc.? And I think it's a well-recognized scale.

When we got the final score, the... counselor asked me if I could re-add it because I was in the low 30s. I said I trusted her. A score of 31 to 40 is severe depression. I needed some very major medication plus a life environment change. What I ended up doing after that, I ended up going on medication, and slowly, we moved my mother-in-law to a long-term home. Daniel eventually found a job and moved out of the house and here we are today. However, it took two or three years of my life to figure out how to get basically in control. Now overall, the big medication is the large lot and property that we own by the Thames River that is my medicine. I spend as much time as possible outdoors with greenery, animals, water, kayaking, vegetables, fruits, all the things that bring me at ease.

Ruby Scott

Miss Ruby Scott was my grade 9 art teacher. In high school, we had to take art. This subject was part of the academic stream to separate programs from the technical stream. The academics were set up to eventually go to university. So here I am, a left-brain person taking art that uses the right brain. I discovered that Ruby Scott and I didn't see the world in the same way. Every time there was some artistic interpretation that had to be done, whether it was pottery or watercolors, there was always a discussion on the approach to take to do the artwork. One assignment was to show how drugs can impact a person's life. We are in the era of hippies and rock and roll at Woodstock. I decided that my watercolor is going to be a plane crashed onto a flat surface with wheels, parts, wings, and tail flying in all directions. I showed the picture to Miss Scott, and she gave me a D plus. I went to her, and in every conceivable way of inappropriate language, I fought and tried my best to get a higher mark. I explained to her that the watercolor represented the impact of a pilot who was on drugs and crashed the plane. Miss Scott would have none of it because she was convinced that I did not do the right artwork to represent the impact of drugs on a person. There were some other incidents that took place, including not really using the pottery oven very well. The entire year, eventually, it got so bad that attitude took over and to prove that I was not really following instructions.

She made me write the final exam in art. It's now June. I'm in the gymnasium with the room full of empty desks and me writing the final exam in art. I had to study the lives of all the great artists, Leonardo, Van Gogh, and Michelangelo. I did end up passing; however, that was my penalty for being arrogant and not following instructions and making life difficult for Miss Ruby Scott. At that time, she had 35 years of experience at the high school. She was a legend. Some of my high school friends still talk about that and how I was able to get under the skin of our art teacher. I thought it was not the right thing to do at the time; however, that was the attitude coming out again. I still think through it, and on one side think I had to prove my point; on the other side, I think, why did you do that? There were so many other ways that you could have passed grade 9 art; instead, I chose the hardest one of all.

Miss Ternan:

English is not my native language, so having that in my brain took me a long time to convert from Italian to English. It took me a long time, for example, to do multiplication in English. I used to do the timetable in Italian in my head, then convert, and then speak in English. As time went on, I had some very interesting experiences in my English. The first one started with the English teacher in grade 9, Phyllis Ternan. She is a lovely person and took an interest in me. I wanted to see if I could finally learn because when I was in grade 9, I'd only been in Canada for four years. One thing that I remember, she was a stickler for punctuation. She marked with quarter-point deductions for tests. One of the tests that we had to do was to write a précis on a book that we read. The book was Moonfleet. It was extremely complicated and hard to read for me, and we had to get it into 500 words. Unfortunately, I had messed it all up. I used many more words because a lot of them were duplicates, trying to make sure that the English fell into the right place. I recall having my meeting with her because I ended up with 4.5 out of 10. After a lengthy discussion, me going back and forth, we finally settled on 4.75. I got an extra quarter mark. To this day, I still remember Ms. Ternan. She was a lovely person because she took an interest in me. However, I still remember how hard she was on me, and maybe there's a lesson to how to learn, how to have someone mark you hard.

My next phase in high school was mastering the English Language. The Merchant of Venice in grade 10 English was a bear. This has a humorous element to it because the main character is Antonio, and he is teamed up with Portia. I remember those two names very well to this day. However, I could not get Ms. Cudney to have me called by Angelo. The entire year, she continued to call me Antonio, to the point where one of my best friends, Kirk, took me aside one day and said, "Angelo, just go with it, and you will be Antonio for all of the rest of grade 10". And to this day, I still chuckle over that. I have been called Antonio by many others since high school.

Pizza Oven

Our 30th anniversary was one of the events that marked our life as we were in the middle of our wonderful time. It was 2010. We had just moved to our house in Pain Court, where we are today.

Daniel's university friends were all together. Our friends were able to come. We got a pizza oven taken control of by Paolo Perciballi and an assistant. We had an accordion player, Armando Bonfiglio, and his band. It was the event that you keep in your mind as one of the best things that we have done. The event was fantastic. What is cool about it is that years later, when we were at the shop where the pizza oven came from, it was still sitting in the back, abandoned.

I saw Paolo and offered him $1,000, and he took it. So, the pizza oven came to our house as a memory and a refurbishment. We're still using it. When the people who refurbished it looked at it, they marveled at how a masterpiece it was of steel on wheels with license plates ready to be towed. It looks like a little hacienda. While we've been using it, we have had some great parties.

Emily Slavik and I spent some time brainstorming the idea of catering pizza parties with the oven. We had it all written up and then realized that insurance companies had no interest in the idea. Leave it to insurance companies to scare anyone from doing anything.

Emily and her family agreed to do a pizza party for the wedding party of our next-door neighbors. That was another event that will live in the ages. They were supposed to start at about 9 o'clock after their meal. They never got going until close to midnight. It's an outdoor event in June. It just dragged on. By the time the pizza was rolling out, the entire crowd was young and drunk. The older crowd had gone home. Emily and her family went through patiently until 2.30 a.m. To this day, we still talk about that event. However, what we took out of that is that our catering business idea for doing pizza parties was abandoned. After seeing how they go, we have parked the idea for pizza party catering. We're waiting for something else to happen. But an event like that is not going to happen again. Emily, Steven, Mya, and Finn are the best catering team ever!

Pizza Oven Fun in 2023

Enrico and Pat

What are the chances of meeting up with Enrico Magnani from Bologna, Italy, while living in Pain Court? There are not that many Italians that live in our town of 500 people. Enrico came to one of my spin classes, and since that time was over, we ended up being in a bit of a bromance. He's the one who delivered all the groceries when I was sick with COVID for 40 days. We've exchanged recipes. He now has his own pizza oven shed at the new house. Through the time that we knew each other, we watched their two children, Bruno and Valentina, grow up. Along with Enrico, his wife Pat was a follower of the spin class and all the great things that we've done in together. Pat is an avid gardener who experiments with vegetables and plants galore. She is the one who brings her plans to my plant hospital when they get too leggy. Unfortunately, they've had to move on in their lives. They moved to Montreal to be with family. They became our children because their children were here so many times and we treated them as our grandchildren. So great friends, great memories stay with you forever. Enrico and Pat, you are good friends. We wish you all the best in your future.

Joe Donais

Our married days are Sarnia began by meeting up with Joe Donais. He is the young man and entrepreneur who sold us our very first house. One summer afternoon, as he was building the house next door to ours, we began a tradition that continued for decades and kept a special bond. I found an overgrown zucchini plant that was in the empty lot next tour. I was about ready to throw it out when Joe stepped and said, "Let me cook it." He made a secret sauce with spices and tomatoes and left it on the barbeque for several hours in an aluminum tray. In the evening, we had an excellent supper followed by a sweet Italian liqueur called Strega. The girls chatted, and we fell asleep! It was the beginning of an Annual Zucchini Fest that continued through the eighties and nineties. Every year the families got together and celebrated the tradition that was started by Joe.

The Immigrants

I am forever thankful to Canada for providing me and our family with everything that we have. The Immigrant story that Canada has worked on and continues to embellish is a success that will be admired years from now as one of the greatest accomplishments of society. My portion of the success story in Canada involves specifically my admiration for all the immigrants that I've worked with and experienced. I will give you some examples of how the immigrants that I've worked with and laughed with embellished our life; the Prochazka family that worked with me in the BASF days came from Czechoslovakia; they left during the communist regime one night; he and his wife took a train to Austria there they were put in a camp while they waited for a country to take them they ended up in Canada both are extremely intelligent individuals that helped me tremendously we've stayed in touch for years their children have grown up and succeeded however that story of two young Engineers leaving their country with nothing and succeeding in Canada is something that I admire them for and is it true reflection of all Canada as help the world.

The next family that I would like to talk about is an engineer, his name is JV. When I was interviewing him during my BASF days, he was applying for a maintenance engineer with nearly 40 years of experience. When I asked them why he wanted to do this for such a low salary and stay in Canada, all he said was, "Angelo, I will take any pay because all I want is for my children to grow up in Canada." he was from Bangladesh. I couldn't believe that he said that he would take a salary so low compared to all others with that seniority. However, it was for his family.

The Nikolov family that I met during my Greenfield days is equally courageous with an immeasurable desire to succeed in terms of Courage. Veselin and his wife, with two daughters, left Bulgaria right after the Soviet regime was being dismantled. He stated that he served in the Russian Air Force and flew combat aircraft during his twenties. The stories that he told me would make any Canadian cringe at the thought of what he was being asked to do by that regime. My admiration for the Veselin family is incredible. Their desire for success and love of our freedoms is evident every time we meet for lunch.

The Bhutanese families of Jamona and Kangri that came to our Gardens are equally incredible as a family that lived in a refugee camp in Tibet for 10 years while waiting to come to Canada. Kangri was the cook at the camp where he married his wife, Chandra. They joined our Garden Club and worked so hard on her plots, keeping them immaculate. One Sunday morning we were treated to a meal all made from our vegetables, Kangri cooked with a propane kit in our garage. I will remember that day forever. To this day, they are in Chatham succeeding very well and all I have done with them is just exchange vegetables. They are so thankful to be here in Canada and have started a community from the refugee camp that got them here. They work so hard the whole family has now purchased a property in a nearby town, and we still stay in touch. It is another success story of how kind are Canadian system is to immigrants to make this great country succeed.

There is one more family that has shown equal courage in their 30s. With two young children Romina and Juan have come from Argentina to look for success and share in the Canadian dream. The kids have learned a new language quickly. Mom and dad have had to switch to another way of life and language. The children are fast adapters and are fluent in English. They remind me so much of the success story that our family went through, however, the differences in their educated professionals. They left their family behind and showed courage to be Canadian and to share in the success of our great country. We ended up in Canada by a strange coincidence. Mom told me that during the war the Canadian soldiers offered her and the other kids candy. She always had a soft spot for Canada.

Dr. Scott and Calculus

I quickly realized that I had gone from a big fish in a small pond in Leamington District Secondary School to the University of

Western Ontario when I was a little fish again. Specifically, calculus was the time that I discovered how small a fish I was. In the first midterm in October, I got a mark of 39 out of 100, while the class average was 37. Dr. Scott, the professor at the time, was the most intimidating person I have ever met. He first handed out the exams by saying that someone got 100, and he announced the name. Then he began announcing in reverse. And many people got 1% for putting their name on the paper. And eventually, it got to everyone. It was humiliating and devastating. I left that class, and as I walked back to the residence, I nearly thought to myself, my life is over because I had come from grades like 90-95%. Peter was a classmate who was walking with me on the way back to my residence from campus. That's the bridge over the Thames River. He nearly lost it, and a few weeks later, I didn't see him in engineering anymore. That was the beginning of, are you going to make it or not? And on top of that, when I went home for Christmas, I didn't tell my mom that I failed my exam. Because when they did the belled the marks, I ended up with a 59. Because the class average was so low, they brought everybody up. Welcome to engineering. Dr. Scott was one of the early hurdles that taught me humility. I needed that person to tame my rebellious persona and bring me down to earth.

Dr. Blackwell

I did get past Dr Scott in first year calculus; however, second year calculus was even more difficult that's when I ran into Dr. Blackwell. I started out the year believing that I was doing okay. It's a full year course, and by my midterm, I had to decide tough decision. Get good marks on my half term courses and worry about Calculus in the second half. After my midterm, my mark in Calculus was in the mid-60s. I now had to choose whether our final exam would be for the entire year or use 33% of it to add to the rest. Use one exam for all the marbles, or end up with a C. During March break, I made the decision to study while everyone else went to Florida for their spring break. I thought it would get through and hopefully get an A. I decided to study like crazy for the entire March. When it came to exam time, I went to Weldon Library at Western for weeks, and all I did was study math. I took wake up pills and was determined to get an A in calculus.

The night before the exam, I studied till 11:00 as it was my normal routine. I tried to fall asleep I could not and by 1:00 a.m. I realized that that night, I was going to be sleepless. I tried everything possible. I ended up getting some splitting headache like a pierced Javelin was in my brain that kept me awake all night. I finally took enough aspirin to be able to fall asleep, maybe for half an hour.

I went to Alumni Hall, where the exam was being held. I met my dear friend Jim, and we went in to begin to write. I also realized that Jim had not had much sleep because that was our main exam; it would make or break us. I wrote the exam. I don't know what happened; all I remember is getting home and crashing. Sheer luck would have it, when I got the final Mark in early May, I ended up with an 82%. To this day, I do not know how I did that! I believe that somehow, some greater force acted on me to get me the mark that I wanted. As I write, I can re-live every minute of April 1976. I now realize that I experienced a migraine headache during the night before the exam. I did not know it then, but later in life, Dr. Blackwell taught me to reach deep within to find what is needed for mental toughness.

Mrs. Mattei:

I just wanted to share a moment of hilarious times with Rosella's mom. When she stayed with us for a little bit before she moved on to a retirement home, one day, I was at work. I got a phone call from Rosella, and she said that mom had been bitten by a bat. I took the call because I was in the middle of doing something at work, and after a while, I realized, wait a minute, this is not a good thing. So, I called my sister, who is a nurse, and said, "This may be a case of rabies." If the bat has rabies, she may have to get rabies shots. I rushed home and ended up taking her to her emergency; it took most of the day to figure out that we had to get a rabies shot kit that comes from the health unit. I got that. The next day, we went to a doctor who administered the rabies shots. The way that works is you get five shots, the first is two sets at one time, and then you must go three more visits to finish them. What just so happens is that the bat bite was on the middle finger. After waiting a bit and going to see the doctor, who knows all about this, he proceeds to take the needle and inject two separate shots in the middle finger. And I can tell you that my mother-in-law, who is 90 at this time, is screaming and going, first, I do not want this. She is in the old country, and I will survive. The doctor went ahead and said, Ma'am, I'm sorry you must take this because I do not want to be responsible for sending a 90-year-old on to the next life because that would not look good. So, we proceeded to get all the shots done. But the most hilarious part was when we left; her middle finger was the size of a hot dog. And she left yelling and screaming the whole time. Saying, this is not the way I want to do this. But we ended up finishing it anyway. The hilarious part is she insisted that the bat had to be picked up because she wanted to save it. And she got a little bite at the end of the finger that we had to take care of. It's still one of those moments that between all the nurses, which would be Elise and my sister Anna and everyone else; at that time, it was a hilarious moment that you never forget. Mrs. Mattei taught me the meaning of Tough!

Elisha:

In my journey to repay mother earth and go carbon neutral our solar panel installation brought a person into my life that made a lasting impact. Elisha Ogbonna came to do the installation and as we struck up a conversation we connected. Elisha came by several times to finish the project and each time he amazed me with his love of life, family and spiritual insights. Elisha was here to see the solar project work very well. He also was present when we discovered the human remains. During the entire time we became friends.

I learned that beyond his electrical engineering skills he loves writing and publishing books. I am still in amazement t his talents. His English language mastery is admirable. I did learn that he learned English going to a well-organized Nigerian schooling system. Elisha sent me one of his published books and inspired me to go ahead and publish the memoirs that I have been working on for years.

Inspiration comes to us in many ways. One way is to meet someone that exudes that trait that you want to emulate, and the rest will happen. I began the journey of book editing with a goal to publish. Elisha gave me some tips and off I went into the black hole of o line editors and publishers. After months of searching and nearly being scammed several times, I called Elisha and regrouped.

His tips helped guide me a lot because it forced me to learn the mechanics. I did learn that when someone gives you ideas that you, they must follow you will always use them as your north star. I am deeply appreciative for the guidance given to me by Elisha for the memoirs you are enjoying.

CHAPTER 11

Career and Life Lessons

Suppose I go through the experiences when I began writing and the parts that you've read; you can tell that it's a combination of true-life experiences as well as a bit of philosophy. It's a combination of all those thoughts, and near the middle to the end, I realized that maybe there is a message that these writings should send to the reader. I'm not sure exactly how to word it. However, I do believe that it goes to the root of our mental health and how we all find our way through life. It's based on our experiences, as well as trying to internalize how we know ourselves. Starting with being a young Italian immigrant to Canada, going through the pressures of being the first and oldest, having to carry the family in all kinds of situations, having to support my mom and my dad and my sisters, going back to the trauma that I had with my bike accident, and also being around my dad, clearly had, even back in the younger days, some signs of depression. Those are the experiences that have made me and brought me to where I am today.

You have read several portions of my story about my mom, and one of the more important lifetime experiences that I had with my mom was her helping my dad with his depression. He got into a small fender bender and ended up losing his driver's license. It was very late. It was in his mid-70s. By that time, things were not going well with Mom's health as well, but she had enough courage to take him through months of depression and eventually recovered, including finding a psychologist who helped him for years with medication. And to this day, I do believe that mom saved my dad's life, one of the reasons why I admire her so much is the glue that kept our family together for years and years. And it culminated with the accident, but it was a long time that she worked with dad to make sure that he kept things together.

That began my running obsession which led me to eventually run the Boston Marathon. During my BASF days, I spent much time in Mexico learning how Mexico works and how much they like Canadians, but they don't really like gringos. So, I ended up being an assigned contact to do many good things in the Mexico experience. After the experience that I had, I started a career move that was called the BASF, called Rationalizing Plants. Basically, I oversaw closing plants that were not making money. It didn't end well because I worked myself out of a job, and that's when I ended up with Greenfield here in Chatham.

My engineering profession is the love of my life. I've learned so much living it. I've contributed by leaving landmarks that will serve and help society. I'm very proud that I was able to choose that profession.

In Chatham, I ran the plant safely, set all kinds of records, and retired. The assignment after retirement was a cannabis new project experience that ended up out of my hands. I was not choosing to go into cannabis. During COVID, we purchased a plant in Minnesota, and I helped start it up, and it's still running today. As I write this, I'm now in gardening mode and basically following the footsteps that I learned from my grandfather back in Italy in the early 1960s. So, that's a short version of the story. That's a short version of the travels of Angelo through time.

When I started at Shell and then moved out west, there was a great future back in the 80s because oil was going to skyrocket. We were planning to build all kinds of new facilities out west. The facility I helped build grew into a massive complex. Scotford now supplies all of Canada with refined products. I am proud to look at it on Google Earth. Sometimes, I zoom in and look at the Hydrocracker unit and picture myself when it was being erected. As time went on, all the plant closures that took place, we faced the decision to go back to our roots in Ontario. It was primarily because of family reasons. At that time, we were trying to adopt, and we just had a small market in Alberta, and that's where BASF came into our life.

The leadership traits that I have listed come from many people who have helped me through my career and personal life. These are not in any order; however, each one of them has added an aspect to my life that guides me. I've carried it to this day. Their influences guide me. In the Shell days, his name was Kevin Hogan; at the time, he was the head of the Scotford project that was approved at around 500 million when it started, and it ended up being 900 million dollars. I recall one time and him talking to our group about the cost overrun. He said that he was asking for an overrun of nearly 400 million dollars; he replied I'm doing this because now we are so committed; we already have spent 400 million in the ground that we can't back out now and leave that money in the ground. To this day,

I still remember the conversation because it showed the determination, vision, and passion not to ever give up.

Marty Cormier hired me a Greenfield, and to this date, we have mutual respect. I'm about 15 years older than he is; however, each time we've met and discussed, we have an admiration beyond anything. It has to do with the trust that we built by working with each other, as well as the respect for different views and how they're accepted even in the most difficult times.

Howard Field is the person that, while we were discussing options that we had in front of us for a business venture, he said, "Angelo, if you are trying to start a fire using a magnifying glass and pointing it to grass, you must keep it focused on that spot for as long as you can, and then the fire will start. Right now, you're moving your magnifying glass repeatedly, and you'll never start a fire". Those words stayed with me, and it's an indication that if you focus on something long enough, you will make it happen. That theme can be carried on to life in general. Patience and perseverance qualities are all necessary to continue your life journey. Patience, I lack, but determination and persistency, especially when faced with difficulty, is called doggedness. I believe I have nurtured doggedness nicely.

Katie Amato showed me the impact and how working together as a team helps us mutually get incredible accomplishments. Katie worked with me for years at Greenfield as my human resources manager, and we developed a relationship, especially when it came to people who worked immensely well. She showed me that being always connected so that the people aspect of a factory never loses focus. She helped me immensely especially as a person that is mostly left brain. Katie was my right brain and that was so wonderful on the soft people complexities that are often gray and not black and white.

Greenfield is a privately owned company that respected everything that I brought to the table with the experience that I brought with them. I started in 2005, the time when it was very early in the company, and I also ended up meeting a boss that I still respect today, and we respect each other immensely. Marty Cormier is a fun loving, focused man with immense integrity. I helped him build a high purity alcohol expansion that turned the company around. I drive by it often. It's tangible and visible and continues to thrive. We still stay in touch, and now we have become friends more than boss and worker. The best part that I have is in his farewell speech that we gave when I retired. He used the line, "Angelo was the best decision that I've ever made in my career." It's endearing and powerful, and I'm so thankful that I met Marty Cormier. The engineering part, I really got a bow on it because when I retired, an award was given with my name on it. It's an engineering high school award that goes to a student that goes to one of the local universities, and that is an annual award that every year, I get to look at a young, bright mind that eventually will go to one of the local universities. You can't put a price on the satisfaction of this appreciation gift.

Marty is an avid Bruins and Patriots fan and is in love with Tom Brady. He enjoys his golf game and outdoors.

We have similar loves for the outdoors and healthy living. We must like each other because I am a Lions and Leafs fan.

December 2017 – Best Boss Ever

This is a form from my boss, Marty Cormier after I retired from Chatham Plant Manager. Twelve years ago, in the fall of 2005, I held the position of Plant Manager at the Chatham site. Our Maintenance and Engineering Manager at that time, Rick Lehoux, had recently been promoted to the GET department, and Katie Amato and I were during recruiting for a replacement.

During the interview process we met several promising candidates, but none had the combination of skills and experience that we were looking for. Then along came Angelo Ligori, a strong candidate with excellent experience, having previously worked with Shell Canada and BASF. There was no question he possessed all the technical skills necessary to do the job; this was clear. Technical fit, however, was only half of the requirement; we were also looking for a dynamic leader who would be a great fit in the organization and have the energy and drive to take us to the 'Next Level".

I still remember his resume, which included a selfie photo from a marathon that Angelo had recently completed. At first, I thought the photo was a little quirky, but I thought to myself, this guy has discipline, energy, stamina, and drive, and those traits will serve him well in the role. We hired Angelo, and as the saying goes, "the rest is history."

During his tenure as Engineering and Maintenance Manager, Angelo helped us resolve long standing performance reliability issues with our Cogen system while preparing the plant for the commissioning and start-up of our first major Industrial Expansion (HPA60). Angelo brought discipline and structure to our engineering processes and helped us get to the "Next Level."

Around the same time that Chatham was starting up the industrial expansion, the company was building our first fuel ethanol plant in Varennes and designing a second fuel ethanol facility in Johnstown. I was heavily involved with supporting the fuel expansion plans and we needed a strong leader to focus on and support the Chatham Plant. Angelo was promoted to the Chatham Plant Manager position in February of 2008, and as the saying goes, "the rest is history."

Over the next nine and a half years, Angelo led the Chatham team through several strategic projects and initiatives while enhancing Chatham's safety culture and its presence in the community. Some of the more notable projects included a second industrial expansion (IA42) and the installation of a second Cogen. Angelo also led the plant through the Truly Greens Farm project which includes the delivery of fermentation CO_2 and dryer waste heat to an adjacent greenhouse growing tomatoes. The heat integration phase of the project will be completed in Q4 of this year. For all of this, I thank you.

Chatham has hosted many visitors over the years, from Customers, Suppliers, Government Officials, Media, Lenders, Shareholders, Peers, and Senior Leadership. Consistently I hear praise when anyone visits Chatham as they are treated first class and are made to feel extra special. This is a direct reflection of Angelo's pride and commitment to Greenfield. He has an amazing ability to make visitors feel welcome and treated with the utmost respect. Angelo has been an outstanding ambassador for the Chatham Facility and for Greenfield Global. For all of this, I thank you.

Angelo has also done a great job of positioning the Chatham Plant for future success, not only on the technical side but also on the people side. Angelo is a strong believer in employee development and promotion. The majority of Chatham's current leadership team was hired, promoted, and developed under Angelo's leadership. He has assembled and developed a strong leadership team that has positioned the plant for tremendous success moving forward. Angelo also introduced programs to develop and grow our future leaders through the Stationary Engineering apprenticeship program and the Engineering Coop program. For all of this, I thank you.

As we look ahead, Angelo will now be taking on a brand-new challenge with the company. As Senior Advisor, Bulk Manufacturing, Angelo will be sharing his vast experience and knowledge to support several projects that will advance many of our strategic initiatives.

Angelo will be working very closely in the areas of: Business Continuity, Long Term Site Plans, Business Optimization, Food Safety Regulations, and Reliability and EH&S Improvement. Angelo will also continue to build and strengthen Chatham's presence in the community, serving as our official representative for local events.

Angelo, I am truly grateful for everything that you have done to lead Chatham through an amazing phase of growth. You have taken Chatham to the "next level." I am equally thankful for your future involvement in many of the strategic initiatives that we have planned and for sharing your experience and wisdom with our next generation of leadership.

Warmest Regards, Marty Cormier

October 2018 – Where is my Car

This trip to Kentucky is a classic Gong show! It started in the morning when I turned the family room TV on, and the video was cooked. Yes, our 10-year-old Sharp Aquos had just died. Of course, Rosella and Mrs. Mattei are in a panic because they will not be able to watch all their cooking shows. Vince was down to babysit, so he was in no mood to deal with that. So, I decided to move the TV from the master bedroom. 2 hours later, the old TV was out, and the new one was working. Most of the time was dialing up and talking to the Bell Satellite help desk to get the signal to come in. It was close to 11:00 by the time all was back in order. Now, I had to pack, get a few emails out, and be on the road to Detroit for a 4:00 p.m. flight. At 12:30 I am backing out of the garage. Of course, I forgot that Vince had his nice BMW parked behind me. Even with the back-up alarm beeping I hit the front driver side hard enough to scuff up the bumper nicely. Obviously, I had way too much on my brain.

As I approached Huron Church to the Ambassador Bridge, the traffic came to a complete stop. After nearly one hour, I finally decided to look on Google maps, showing one more hour to get across the bridge. Now I am in a panic and decide to take the tunnel. After a sweat filled drive through all the detours in Detroit, I finally got to HI 94. It's now nearly 3 p.m., and the traffic is backed u because the tracks that were being held up are finally also hitting HI94. I made it to the plans as the class's last call as they called my name for boarding. I was the last one on and got a widow seat beside a guy who was 230 lbs at 6 foot 3. The plane had been sitting with no AC on a hot, humid day because the auxiliary power was not working. The AC would come on when the plane was started up. The man beside me had a face the color of a tomato and beads of sweat on his forehead. I was equally on fire after my long ride.

This is a blog from Connie Deyo, a Greenfield workmate. "After a long travel day yesterday, it was awesome to be greeted at the hotel by three of my Engineering friends, Angelo Ligori, Brian Gartley, and Chris Bradt. This morning, after meeting for breakfast Angelo suggested I could ride in with him to get caught up. He failed to mention that he had no recollection of where he parked his rental car! After walking around aimlessly, we knew we had an issue. Since time was of the essence and we couldn't run a full Kaizen, my friend Angelo decided he'd simply hit the panic button on his key fob. Other travelers were enjoying this comic routine, so of course, Angelo engaged in conversation with them, so much so that he walked past the car and had to hit the panic button a second time! Never a dull moment when we are together! "

On my way back, the weather was still humid and stormy. We circled over Detroit for about one hour because of passing storms. When we landed, I saw a text from sister Stefania that said there was a tornado coming toward Chatham. I called her and told her I was in Detroit, and she mentioned that the weather was bad with the wind gusts and heavy downpours. As I reached the top of the Ambassador Bridge and looked east, I could see lightning bolts and a narrow band of light sky just above the horizon. It all looked very scary.

When I got to the house and opened the front door, Vince and his dog Stella looked at me as if I was their savior. The storm had caused a power failure, and all the battery power, security, and clock alarms were going off. Stella's eyes were the size of Tim Bits. Vince said it was like a freight train going by the house just 30 minutes ago. Mrs. Mattei was pacing like a lost soul, and Rosella was under the covers hiding. I tried to get to sleep at 11:30 p.m. and recapped the last 24 hours. I finally understood why I could not remember where I parked my rented car at the Marriot in Kentucky.

March 2019 – Where is my dad?

It was at Kaya's confirmation party that Stefania heard from Uncle Tony about Dad being at Leamington Hospital Emergency. As the story goes Dad was coming from Carmen's catering, and as he tried to start the truck, he was seen by a passer-by looking very confused and unable to start the truck. He was taken by ambulance to an emergency, where he was stabilized. After a few hours, he called Uncle Tony and went back home without telling any of his kids. It became an atypical day in the life. After we found out, it was clear that Dad needed some intervention.

We took him to a cardiologist after meeting with Dr. Leong (his doctor). Dr. Leong is likely one of the most complicated doctors I have seen in a long time, and I had to figure things out myself. The cardiologist recommended that Dad stop driving and make medication changes to get his weight down and reduce his congestive heart condition. Stefania did a great job to get Dad to Chartwell Retirement Home which is just across the street from our house. The Ford ranger went to a very nice man from Milton. The house is in the process of being sold to the Neighbour.

On March 15th, I had the plan to have a new Medic Alert for Dad and meet with the neighbor at the house to discuss the sale. At 4:30, I met with the Security One salesperson. I got the unit and went to meet with the home RPN to set up how to give it to Dad on Monday. After discussing the plan with Jennifer McLean, she told me that Dad was sick with the flu in his room, and the room was quarantined. She suggested that I leave him be. I listened to her and headed to the house just across the street. As I walked to the car, it started raining as it was raining off and on all day. As I got closer to the hose, I could see a man, with a walked walking to our house. In disbelief, I realized it was Dad. He told me that he came to get the mail and feed the rabbits. I was not pleased with him and gave him a ride back to the home. As I headed to the front door, he asked me to take him back through his room patio door.

On my way back home after settling down, I replayed the scene in my head in a comic version. So, Angelo has this great plan to get Dad to wear the medic alert by making sure that the nurses give it to him so that he will not resist. He is known for not listening to me. However, Dad outsmarts me by going out the back door and not signing out of the home like he is supposed to. So much for all my planning and worrying, I have been outsmarted by an 85-year-old dad.

April 2019 – Siblings Day

While looking thought all the pictures from 24 Melrose Avenue that we are about ready to sell after 50 years, I picked up this beauty of a picture. It's the one that really jumped out among all the others.

Anna has that beautiful smile that I over now and loved when she was first born. According to my mom, I was not happy at the beginning. Apparently, I walked around blaming Mom every time Anna got attention and called her out because Anna was always crying and got all the attention. I eventually took a liking to Anna and carried her on my back to get her around faster. We were 6 and 2. Anna's signature picky nature came out when she could not decide to eat either rice or pasta soup. Anna has continued to compliment me with her caring and nursing nature to this day. She helped me so much when Rosella got sick especially when Daniel needed looking after. On the humorous side, she is the one who recommended I take Nonna Mattei to get rabies shots when she was bitten by a bat. Love you, Anna!

Toni is the cutie that came about when I was 8. She was the most fun when I was using both her and Anna for target practice with my bamboo stick spear with a fork at the end. She was a bit slower, and her feet were nice and pudgy. Bet's memory of Toni was visiting her at the University of Windsor residence. Her room was a combination of a party store, gift shop, and habitat. Coming from the engineer in me, I envied her social butterfly nature. Seeing her get a Master's in Sociology was a proud moment. Toni's health challenges have motivated me to focus on my own health. I will never forget visiting her just after starting work at Shell in 1978. She was admitted to London University Hospital with her first diabetic attack. The memory of such a young, helpless person that she was is still with me to this day. I got to love my Toni.

Stefania has a special bond with me. She was born in 1968 when I was in high school and had to face my friends asking what are your parents doing having a baby now? She grew up watching Kirk, Spike, Dave, Herb, and Paul playing poker and smoking cigars. She had a crush on Spike. We have a father daughter relationship more than a brother sister. She leaned her football from watching me follow the NFL. She got her name because when dad wanted to name her Joanna, I had a crush on a girl at school named Stephanie Casper. Stefania has continued to be my "wingman" sister. It's the combination of age spread personality connection, our mom, and our life experiences that have kept us best friends.

In my teens and twenties, I went through the discoveries of life. It was a time of endless, innocent experiences. It was a time of immortality with a touch of reckless behavior. In my thirties time was hurried and rushed. In my forties, I had the experience with Rosella's health, the experience with adopting, and the experience with my own mortality.

Fifty was the beginning of reflection and insight. I used endorphins as the cure for all the ailments that I had to deal with. I must say that that decade was life changing. When I reached my fifties, I realized that there was more to life than just chasing something that was tangible and material. Slowly, my life purpose became clearer. I realized with the events around me and watching my elders face mortality there must be more to life. I have run Boston at fifty. My career is very satisfying yet the two people in my life need me. It's at this time that I chose not to spread myself too thin. Rosella and Daniel are the ones that remain my purpose in life.

The sixties decade went by in a flash. Suddenly, I was the older that was looked at for wisdom. I gave my view pint and people listened. I often thought that it was just a viewpoint, yet it was a deciding one. Not sure how I got to that point, but I did. The home on a peaceful property meant so much more because I now understood myself as linked with nature. As my peers did their travels, I peacefully kayaked on the Thames Rives and watched fish jump out of still waters.

In my seventies I've reached the point now when giving back to family and the community means everything. Being a caregiver and finding peace with nature is my happy place. Marathons and endorphins are now a memory, and for a good reason. Arthritis is now my friend. An afternoon nap is gold.

Plants, water, and fresh air are my medications without the intensity of running. I can clearly say that peace and a sense of self-accomplishment have arrived. It's a feeling that I've had to get to all on my own, by all the experiments and all the experiences that I went through to get me to this point. Medication is not a fix. I went through antidepressant medication, and it numbed me. It took what I heard one say, the red Ferrari, out of me, and I was a flat Volkswagen that absolutely had zero personality and zero color. Where I'm at today is where I can retain all those things and yet be at peace and use Mother Nature, vegetables, and all the surroundings that I experience every day here. I'm able to mentor Alex and his young family that is now farming on the lot that next to us. The opportunity to mentor another person who is attentive and wants to learn is a rare find. We talk daily, and it's a wonderful feeling. It's gone full circle because I was that person when I was back in Italy chasing my grandfather around. So, it's an amazing experience that I can share with you, and it all has to do with finding ourselves. And that's not something that one does in days. It's in decades. However, it does work. After you read these stories, I'm hoping that it helps just one of you to do something better for mankind and for themselves.

After all my experiences, I am giving back to the community. As a Board Director of the Chatham Kent YMCA Foundation, I will champion healthy living, especially for our youth. I will do it if my health lasts. As Board Director of the Chatham Kent Health Alliance, I plan to make a difference to the health and well being of our community. Eventually I will end up needing their care. It's called long term planning.

I am a learner and common-sense thinker. I would like to make a difference to my loved ones, our community and humanity. I believe that life is beautiful because I can look past the imperfections.

Regrets are not part of my chemistry. Impossibilities intrigue me. Visualization of any task to get done is my magic. A personable approach is my secret to life and relations.

CHAPTER 12

Back to My Roots

Our life is like getting a brand-new motorcycle. We all get the same tank of gasoline. Some tanks are full, and some are partly empty. We don't know how much gas there is in the tank. It's important to ride along so that we use up every drop of gas. We should not leave a single drop in the tank. I got this analogy from my cousin Gaetana in my hometown of Pofi. I used a few drops of gasoline in August 2025 when I decided to return to my native town. It was necessary so that I could reconnect with Uncle Luigi. The reception was one of the most spiritually fulfilling events of my life. I experienced life surrounded by family that opened every aspect of their life to me.

In August 2025, nearly 60 years after leaving in 1966, I returned to the lane of my childhood in Pofi—this time driven by my first cousin Luciano, son of Zio Luigi.

The purpose of my visit was deeply personal: to reconnect with my roots and spend time with Luigi, who is facing serious health challenges due to a heart condition. As someone ten years younger than Zio Luigi—and with my father being ten years older than him—I felt a responsibility to help preserve the Ligori legacy.

Luciano, born in December 1966 just months after I left Italy, has remained a strong link to my heritage. His connection to our family and homeland has always been meaningful to me.

The lane leading to the farmhouse where I was born still exists, now paved, unlike the dirt path I once walked as a child. It's the same path where I accidentally set fire to our haystack over six decades ago. Via Forestella, which connects to the laneway, is also paved now. As we passed the rocky slope where I once crashed my bike, vivid memories came rushing back. Luciano paused to let me take it all in.

This journey was more than a visit—it was a return to my formative years, a reconnection with the innocence and boldness of youth that shaped who I am today.

The favourite place that I used to go was a nice tour that we took with my cousins. The flowing stream that once was is now filled in; there are only a few pools of water that is murky. Trees are big and canopies over, the thistles and wild blackberries cover the walk. There were eels and fish that I used to go to and all the pools of water. Now they are all gone. I swam in a little waterfall area that is now filled in. 60 years later things have changed as Mother Nature does. My cousins had not been down that path in years. They came along with me as my personal guide. Even they were amazed at the changes. Gaetana who is very aware of our surroundings did mention that climate change may be responsible for the drying up of streams

Franco's bar where I used to go and get my gelato as I walked home from school it's still there. The new owner is Matteo. I said hi to him as we had a cappuccino and looked around and recognized that they've changed the bar. However, I could still visualize the pool table that was once there. It's gone now but it's quite etched in my brain.

The church where I was baptized is now San Pietro's convent. The many churches that were there back in my day are closed There are only two that are attended now and four that are closed. That is also a sign of how we progressed in the very transient times of the Catholic religion.

Two farmhouse buildings are quite memorable and still there in pieces. The outhouse and the family kitchen are still there standing. The kitchen roof has collapsed but the thick walls are still standing. The pictures I took will be my memories.

The person that was also in the car with me and came to the airport to pick me up is my second Cousin Simone. He is the son of Gaetana, one of my other cousins and daughter of Zio Luigi. Simone has a PhD in Computer Science. His savvy in AI technology showed me so much about what's happened since I left Italy nearly 60 years ago. Simone and I connected very well because of our Technical and Engineering background. He works remotely with a team then goes to locations to launch automation of businesses. We discussed a new way of remote work in a peaceful town like Pofi where life is stress free compared to Milan, London, etc. He is the one that helped me book the flight back to Canada after Air Canada went on strike while I was in Italy which is a story all by itself.

Gaetana is the cousin that entertained me, cooked, did my laundry and brought everybody to our original homestead. She did and it's so much to make sure that the connection this time was very special. She brought all the cousins she brought schoolmates of mine to the house. She brought friends and showed me life in its simplicity in my hometown. We visited Konad, which is the main grocery chain. Sara was working the deli counter, and we got to visit. She took me to the wholesale warehouse to get good deals. Gaetana had a great haggling encounter with the owner while buying 5 Kilo of English cucumbers. He was having a bad day, and I watched the classic Italian hand waving moments. She won the argument. It was clear he was having a bad day because he took one cucumber away from the box that had about 25. We decided to call him " Uomo Arrabiato" or the angry man. Gaetana made a connection that will stay with us for a good long time. We both love the outdoors. She has a great garden, flowers, fruit trees like figs, purple plums, olives, grapes, persimmons and peaches to name a few.

Gaetana is a person that loves the outdoors. The family locks after all the pets; she has two dogs Hugo and Rudy as her protector. She has turtles, chickens, cats, every imaginable vegetable while keeping the house going. Daughter Sara is at home and works at Konad. Sara is the house helper and supports mom. Sara is 28 and mom casually mentioned marriage at that point Sara laughed. Simone is almost 30 and is also living at home.

 While doing all this Gaetana cuts hair for the family and friends. She rides a scooter to get around. She looks after my uncle and aunt who are now in Rome and don't come to Pofi often. She looks after all the maintenance of the house. The day that I was there she was having a gate installed, dealing with contractors, dealing with wholesalers, dealing with just about everyone that you can imagine and is the classic example of a person that is self-made. It is the reason we relate.

The other person that should be mentioned because he remains the main connection to my roots in Italy is Luciano. Luciano has a son Lorenzo who is currently training to be a Carabiniere just like dad. Luciano took me to the station where he is now the chief of police in a town nearby coffee called Arce. In Arce he presented me with a T Shirt that has the QR code of Pofi Coordinates. He gave it to me because I mentioned that my trip to Italy was only so see Pofi. He wants everyone to know where it is located from now on. He lives on one floor of the station as well as the whole office at the police station has about 10 people and he showed me all his friends all the police team with pride was immensely demonstrated. Luciano arranged tours of Florence, Castro, Monte Cassino and Piana Delle Orme Museo (Latina War Museum).

The Florence trip was special because Luciano lived there when he was serving as a police constable. He knows all the back roads, all the things to do and not to do.

Thank God because the day that we went it was 37 Celsius and although it was fantastic to see all the historic monuments, it was full of tourists, and he was able to navigate all through the city and the highlights around the overwhelming tourists. The Florence trip memory is the Persil sunglasses that I got because I was told by my cousins that I need to have some cool Italian glasses. Buying them was an experience as I learned the art of haggling. After much talking to the sales lady in broken Italian and English, I was able to get 10% discount and the 14% VAT rebate for tourists.

Luciano took us to Castro Dei Volsci, the town where his wife Patrizia was born. It's a high peak that can view the panoramic 360 degrees of all the areas that I grew up in. It's a classic tourist attraction because it's nearly a thousand years old and it has so much history there that everywhere we walked we could see history. The day I spent with Patrizia and Luciano in Arce was special because I got to appreciate life in a police station. I got to meet Luciano's team. Go to see the comradery of a day in their life. The station has several floors, one of which is the residence for Luciano and Patrizia. The station overlooks the valley with breathtaking views. We had some precious time one on one over a meal before heading out to Montecassino. Patrizia treated me to a classic pasta meal.

Monte Cassino where the cathedral is on the monastery is quite an amazing tour that we took. They have a small Museum but dates to thousands of years ago including all the artifacts that were kept after the monastery was destroyed by the allies to get the Nazis out of that town. The carpet bombing is well documented in many history books on World War II. During the visit Patrizia shared her expertise about the history. Patrizia speaks very good English as part of her job as a travel agent. She and Luciano have remained my close connections.

Visiting the Latina war museum has all the history of the area going back to the early twenties. The amazing part is although Mussolini is considered a terrible person when sided with Hitler and caused so much grief for mankind; he was responsible for reclaiming the land around Latina that today feeds the entire area from Naples to Florence. It was all swamps before it was reclaimed. The museum has an amazing display showing the reclamation. Latina is still a vegetable fruit basket of the area and there was so much work there that was done through all the efforts of Mussolini and the time where he was doing good deeds for Italy. There are still people that remember the accomplishments. The bad side of him is indescribable. When I saw the train displays that were used to deport Jewish people from Italy to the death camps I got chills.

Two memorable school friends that I met were Franco Ligori. He remembered saying goodbye to me when we left for Italy. We talked for a good long time. We are the same age. Franco told me stories of his life and including his recent bout with shingles and we laughed over that because we are at the age now, we can compare pains as humans. Franco is intelligent and practical. He stayed in Pofi working in local factories because of poverty. His potential for a successful career was never. In Canada I was able to use it. We had good laughs about all the running around that we did at school, and it was so memorable because he remembered even more than I did.

Another schoolmate I met is Antonietta, who lived three houses next door. I recall she was a bit of a tomboy. She recalled all the running around that we did on the farm back in the late 50s early 60s before I came to Canada. It was quite memorable and again she remembered a lot more than I did and it brought me back to the old days. One thing that I do remember is their house had the only TV in the area. When President John Kennedy was killed, I remember all the area farmers went to see the funeral that was shown on the only TV at Antonietta's house. I still remember that room to this day packed with teary eyed people.

Another memorable moment was seeing my cousin Massimo. The last time I saw him was 26 years ago when I spent a weekend with BASF. Massimo was young and single. He was playing guitar, and he was traveling the world. He now has a daughter who is a concert pianist and a guitar genius son with his own YouTube channel. Massimo speaks very good English. He picked up the guitar and played Neil Young; his favorite folk singer and he played several tunes that brought us back to the common days that we all both liked. He came from Puglia which is about 250 km away. It is Gaetana that pulled everybody together that was probably one of the best surprises that I got. Massimo owns a Parquet flooring business.

The highlight of my visit was the recently opened Museum of archeology in Pofi. It houses the oldest fall called Uomo Ceprano it was discovered recently a few kilometers from Pofi. It comes with controversy, because the excavation site is at the border between the rival town of Ceprano and Pofi. The museum has now grown into quite a reputable destination because it houses all the other ancient history including the first remaining tusks and skull of what the first elephants were not the mammoth that lived in the area through our history. The museum during this time of the year where everybody's on vacation was closed. Simone called his friend Marco Savarese and asked if they could open the museum just for me. Three guides came to open the museum. We spent 2 hours in the museum one on one being taken through every detail of the museum as it was one of the best experiences I've ever had. The tour guides are very young, but they were very proud and interested in what they must show. They put me on their Facebook page with a note saying that a past Pofi resident from years ago came from Canada to tour the museum.

I made a connection with Marco Savarese who's the deputy mayor. He told me a story that is eerie because he showed me a picture of Lorenzo Ligori who was killed during World War II. A Moroccan soldier killed him because he was protecting the ladies from being raped. What I do remember is walking a white cross on a property next to our farmhouse. I always wondered why that white cross was there. My mom told me her version of what happened. When Marco showed me a picture of the headstone it closed out a memory that seemed unreal and answered why that was there. It was finally closed out during my visit in 2025. If you wait long enough you will get an answer to something that you never understood when you saw it. Time heals everything.

While talking, I also learned that Marco is a distant cousin from the Ligori great, great Grandfather. The homestead where I grew up was once owned by my Great Grandfather Bartolomeo and passed to him by his father Domenico or my Great, Great Grandfather. My great, great, great Grandfather born in around 1790 owned all the lands that are now divided into tiny parcels. There are numerous Ligori Families that no longer consider themselves related because of time. It explains why Marco Savarese mentioned we are related, likely over 8 generations.

On the Gori side I met Zia Giovannina. She is the mother of cousins, Antonietta, Margherita and Carla. She is 98 years old and after several repeats she remembered me as Angelino which is amazing. Antonietta is now keeping with her mom. Margherita lost her husband a year ago and is still having trouble moving on. Daughter Carla is in Canada, and I shared my visit with her when I got back. These moments are what define life as a transition.

The visit with Ivano and Rosanna Ivano was equally amazing. Ivano is my cousin on the Gori side. Ivano was a finance officer well versed in everything that's going on in economics. Rossana is a professor at the local University; they live in a well-to-do area near Bracciano. They appreciated the gifts that I brought that are all from Aboriginal Nation stores that I bought here in Canada because I didn't want to bring anything that was made in China. They loved it and Rosanna especially is so fascinated with Aboriginal roots in Canada. We talked for hours about what's going on. We talked about the First Nations current situation with burial sites that were discovered. She is very well informed and has so many questions. We talked till past midnight. The aboriginal connection started when I shared our human remains story.

Ivano is equally informed on our roots. We shared some thoughts about why Italy is the way it is divided, very poor south of Rome and very wealthy in the Milan area. The GDP of the Milan area is equal to the EU wealthy nations. We rode bikes to a volcanic hot spring. We went swimming at the Mediterranean Sea, which is 20 minutes from his house. We got the snorkels on, and he showed me things that are near where he lives. The pieces of sand that were being kicked around by my feet were full of artifacts including Etruscan pottery and mosaic pieces. I took two pieces with me. They are nearly 2,500 years old, so I just give the idea of what history is in Italy. While snorkeling, Ivano found a nail that was used to put Roman ships together. He also found an earring that was brass and flattened. One could tell that that was used as an earring because you could see where there was a stone. I brought these artifacts as a memory back to Canada.

Some of the things that we learned are the same as we have here in Canada. Parents are concerned about their young children and what they will do. Older people are showing signs of slowing down. Youngsters grow up and parents are reminding them because they're not doing things the old way. The customs that I brought from Italy to Canada are long gone because they have moved on. They have all the amenities that we have today. Most of the youngsters were on cell phones and sharing WhatsApp and all the stories that we have.

The common trend in Italy is to live at home to nearly 40. Sara and Simone are on that path especially given the way mom spoils them. Cousin Gianna has one son Alessandro. Luciano and Patrizia have Lorenzo. They are following the flat population growth that has been with Italy for the last generation. Pofi has the same population it had when we left 60 years ago.

The next generation aspires for more, but they all say that Italians like it the way things are. There are signs that their desire to accomplish exists but it's slow. Simone is a great example. Lorenzo is pursuing an engineering degree. Alessandro has learned perfect English and is top of his high school class entering Physics at the University of Rome. Ivano's daughter Giulia is an internal medicine doctor. The signs are there for a bright future.

"Ferragosto" is the biggest holiday in Italy, on August 15th the entire country shuts down. It dates to the old days when farmers took a break from their hard work to rest and party. I chose to be in Pofi and experience it for myself. The day is all about food and relaxing. The meal that was arranged by all the ladies was one of the most special meals I've ever had. All the family were gathered to share all the great dishes that I Gaetana prepared with her family. The food is all mostly vegetarian. Olive oil salt pepper, rosemary, parsley and onions are the staples. Pasta was tortellini with a blush sauce, roasted chicken, green beans, tomato salad and fried peppers were the main dishes. Figs, watermelon and purple prunes were the fruit. Local bakery sweets were served up and of course a local red wine.

That is a classic Italian meal in the area. It's normally at between 3 to 4 pm.

At the table were Uncle Luigi, Zia Assunta, Gaetana, Simone Sara, Gianna, Antonio, Alessandro, Patrizia, Lorenzo, Luciano, Franca, her mom Eleonora, her son Stefano, cousin Massimo that was a group that came to share the special meal.

The talk that I had with Zio Luigi after we were done eating explained was the history of the early 60s and what happened to the Ligori family at the homestead. The four brothers that were there in the late 50s went down to just Luigi by 1966 when we left for Canada. Domenico left for work to go to Novara in 1960. Antonio went to Rome in 1963, and Zio Luigi remained at the homestead. He has kept the place until today. As time went on Zio added to the house, Antonio built another house right next door. Domenico came back to refurbish the Farmhouse, but it's not finished because he passed away in 2017.

Zio Luigi also recollected one of the most dramatic moments that happened to him, the passing of our grandmother Italia. Coincidentally she died of a heart attack while having her Ferragosto meal in 1974. Zio remembers it clearly. He said, "she took her last breath close to midnight after eating". She leaned to one side and gasped one last breath. Zio had a very quivering voice as he told this story tears came to his eyes, and he stopped forget to catch his breath. I could tell as if he lived that moment again. I'm not sure how this coincidence happened but he told me this story today in 2025 that happened in 1974 on the same night. I now know exactly how and when exactly when my grandmother passed away. I spent all my early days with her and loved her then as I do now.

One event that happened during my trip was a validation of human behaviour. Human values and traits are present no matter what country you are in. In Italy my cousin Ivano mentioned a viewpoint to me as we drove to the snorkeling beach on the Mediterranean. He said as we exchanged life experiences "intelligent people are always questioning and looking for answers while stupid people always have answers". He went on to say that he always asking questions and never has enough information to decide. He said that even in his retirement years he feels that he does not have many answers'. I thought about what he said because it's exactly how I view myself. By the way I consider myself confused and not intelligent.

I head the same words from a young lady as I was coming back on the bus from the Toronto airport. On the bus I met a young lady that was headed for Detroit airport. Chinua is her name, and she is from Alabama. We struck up a conversation, and she mentioned almost the same view point she has on human behaviour when it comes to intelligence vs. stupidity. The topic came up as she expressed her disbelief that Alabama voted form Donald Trump. She said that even though Alabama has a great deal of poverty; people were swayed to vote for Trump. She knows that the voters were brainwashed to think that Trump was going to look after the poor people. She also said the exact same words "intelligent people always question why things are and remain with open minds. However, stupid people that always have an answer voted for Trump. These two opposites define how thinkers remain open minded while nonthinkers take the easy road by choosing based on few facts.

I showed the visit pictures to my dad. His brother Luigi and the farmhouse he could remember. I could see the mile on his face. I could tell that for that moment he was happy. Mission accomplished as the saying goes.

The Pofi visit was special for another reason. Rosella got to spend time with Anna and Stefania. They provided care that was new and special. My sisters got to appreciate all that is needed for Rosella. Brother Vince also got to spoil Rosella and experience a special time with her. Rosella equally appreciated the break from our routine. We may have started a new trend for future years.

The Pofi visit prompted my second Cousin Stefano to visit us in 2026. During my Pofi visit we connected with our love for the outdoors and small towns. Stefano will be staying with us and helping as a farm hand at Country Market Gardens that is at the lot next to our house. It will be the beginning of a new relationship and another chapter of Life.

www.ingramcontent.com/pod-product-compliance
Lightning Source LLC
Chambersburg PA
CBHW071725120626
46550CB00002B/392